Jakub Drábik (Ed.)

Operation Danube Reconsidered

The International Aspects of the Czechoslovak 1968 Crisis

With a foreword by Peter Bielik

Jakub Drábik (Ed.)

OPERATION DANUBE RECONSIDERED
The International Aspects of the Czechoslovak 1968 Crisis

With a foreword by Peter Bielik

Bibliografische Information der Deutschen Nationalbibliothek
Die Deutsche Nationalbibliothek verzeichnet diese Publikation in der Deutschen Nationalbibliografie; detaillierte bibliografische Daten sind im Internet über http://dnb.d-nb.de abrufbar.

Bibliographic information published by the Deutsche Nationalbibliothek
Die Deutsche Nationalbibliothek lists this publication in the Deutsche Nationalbibliografie; detailed bibliographic data are available in the Internet at http://dnb.d-nb.de.

Cover image © Peter Bielik

This work was supported by the Slovak Research and Development Agency under the contract No. APVV-15-0349 "Individual and Society – their mutual reflexion in historical process".

ISBN- 978-3-8382-1554-9
© *ibidem*-Verlag, Stuttgart 2021
Alle Rechte vorbehalten

Das Werk einschließlich aller seiner Teile ist urheberrechtlich geschützt. Jede Verwertung außerhalb der engen Grenzen des Urheberrechtsgesetzes ist ohne Zustimmung des Verlages unzulässig und strafbar. Dies gilt insbesondere für Vervielfältigungen, Übersetzungen, Mikroverfilmungen und elektronische Speicherformen sowie die Einspeicherung und Verarbeitung in elektronischen Systemen.

All rights reserved. No part of this publication may be reproduced, stored in or introduced into a retrieval system, or transmitted, in any form, or by any means (electronic, mechanical, photocopying, recording or otherwise) without the prior written permission of the publisher. Any person who does any unauthorized act in relation to this publication may be liable to criminal prosecution and civil claims for damages.

Printed in the EU

Contents

Preface *by Peter Bielik* 7

01. Introduction 9

02. Reflections on 1968 and its Legacies 13
    Jacques Rupnik

03. The Prague Spring and the Evolution of the Position of
    Leonid Brezhnev 23
    Alexander Stykalin

04. Limits of Washington's Position Towards the Invasion of
    Czechoslovakia in the Summer of 1968 35
    Slavomír Michálek

05. Yugoslavia and Czechoslovakia During 1968 49
    Ljubodrag Dimić

06. Towards Military Intervention. Prague Spring and Party
    Representatives in Hungary 67
    Miklós Mitrovits

07. The Communist Authorities and Polish Society in the Face of
    the Prague Spring and the Intervention in Czechoslovakia in 1968 89
    Mirosław Szumiło

08. The Bulgarians and the Prague Spring, 1968 109
    Mihail Gruev

09. Operation "Danube" 119
    Michal Štefanský

10. The Prague Spring and the Warsaw Pact Invasion of Czechoslovakia
    in 1968 as Reflected in the "Western" Historiography 129
    Jakub Drábik

11. Conclusion 159

Selected Sources 163

Preface

My father Ladislav created in August 1968 a set of photographs of the Warsaw Pact troops' invasion to Czechoslovakia. Among these, the famous *Man with bare chest before an occupation tank*—a picture that spread around the world and before being almost completely forgotten. Just like the story of the occupation of Czechoslovakia.

The largest military operation after World War Two has been underestimated for a long time as an insignificant part of history and the most recognisable picture of a Slovak author wandered around the world nameless. However, the truth lay somewhere in the memory of Slovaks and Czechs, while justice for that truth awaited its moment. This came in the year 1989.

The exhibitions of my father's photographs revealed the true face of the occupation. Justice showed itself in the trials in Germany as well as in Slovakia. The pictures of August 1968 became, together with the name of their author, a part of our visual memory and cultural heritage. However, in order to pay the debt to our history and our ancestors, it is necessary to answer also the questions of the causes of the occupation beginning with the word *Why* …?

Why were the Soviets so scared of the Prague Spring?

Why did they send such an unreasonably large, half-a-million strong army?

Finally, why did they name this military intervention after the river Danube?

The answers to these questions were hidden in the archives belonging both to the countries who were our aggressors and to those who had been our allies. Together, also thanks to the work of our non-profit organization, these answers appear in the pages of the book you are holding in your hands right now. Can you find them in the texts of the writers from Serbia, Russian Federation, Romania, Hungary, Bulgaria and other countries? Will these new pieces of information be an inspiration for you in your search for truth about August 1968 in the future?

I do hope so …

Peter Bielik
Head of Camera Obskura, n.o.

01
Introduction

At 11 o'clock in the evening of 20th August 1968, after the signal "Vltava," the armies of four Warsaw Pact countries, the Soviet Union, Poland, Bulgaria and Hungary, crossed the borders of Czechoslovakia. While Romania and Albania refused to participate, East German forces, except for a small number of specialists, did not participate in the invasion because they were ordered from Moscow not to do so. By August 25th, there were 27 invasion divisions in full combat status in Czechoslovakia, over 6000 tanks, and almost 1000 military aircrafts. Over a hundred Czechoslovakian civilians were killed and approximately 500 seriously wounded during the occupation. The invasion successfully stopped Alexander Dubček's Prague Spring liberalisation reforms and strengthened the authority of the authoritarian wing within the Communist Party of Czechoslovakia (KSČ). Literally overnight the Czechoslovak experiment was transformed from living reality into history.

Apart from distressing domestic reforms, especially the decentralization of administrative authority, the more important reason for the Soviet-led Warsaw pact intervention were the signs of a shift in Czech foreign policy that Soviets feared might weaken the position of the Bloc in the Cold War. In regards to foreign policy, the "new course" of Czechoslovakia foresaw wider cooperation with the world, especially with West Germany. Czechoslovakia also sought to loosen its bonds with Warsaw Pact and Comecon, the organization established to facilitate and coordinate the economic development of the Soviet bloc, and gradually showed less and less enthusiasm for the Soviet assistance to the third world countries in a bid to establish its influence there. There was a fear in Moscow that all this could eventually mean that Czechoslovakia might drift away from the communist bloc towards neutrality. This might be followed by Hungary and Poland, slowly undermining the Soviet position in Germany and possibly even losing its buffer zone in Europe.

A decisive faction of the Soviet leadership felt that what was at stake was nothing less than the power balance in Europe—and by extension, potentially the world. That faction saw no other option than a military intervention. Leonid Brezhnev, who did not regard the choice of Alexander Dubček as the successor of Antonín Novotný as problematic in the beginning was subsequently very disappointed. With every liberalizing step in Prague, Moscow grew ever more uneasy. By July 1968, Moscow had come to the conclusion that events in Prague were spinning out of the Party's control and something has to be done. However, Brezhnev feared his rivals in the Soviet elite, who could use against him any weakening of the Communist power in Czechoslovakia, more than the inevitable international outrage that would be caused by the occupation. After hesitations which lasted some months, he made a choice in favour of the occupation.

Although the Soviet Union's action successfully halted the pace of reform in Czechoslovakia, it had unintended consequences for both the unity of the Communist bloc and establishing the new Soviet foreign doctrine. The invasion helped established a so-called Brezhnev Doctrine, that—based on the assumption that a challenge to Socialist rule in one part of the Soviet bloc was a threat to the whole enterprise—justified Moscow's intervention in any country where it felt Communist rule was under threat.

The Warsaw pact intervention, however, did not spark an important international crisis. The division of Europe between superpowers was confirmed and a new version of east-west "détente," based on that understanding, could be launched. Given the exhausting American involvement in the Vietnam War, the Soviets assumed (correctly) that the United States would not intervene and would make do with the condemnation of the invasion. Lyndon B. Johnson cancelled a planned summit meeting with Brezhnev, but this was something that Soviets expected and they concluded that maintaining the control over the Eastern Bloc was more important. Thus, the invasion was completed without any direct intervention from the West or NATO. Similarly, attempts in the United Nations to pass a resolution that would condemn Warsaw pact action were vetoed by the USSR and slowly died away.

This book focuses attention on the international context of the 1968 crisis in Czechoslovakia. Its chief aim has been to bring together experts from within as well without Central Europe and to ignite or—perhaps, better—to re-ignite an international discussion about the Prague spring, its origins, its unfolding, its aftermath and—most importantly—its international context. The debate and historiography regarding the Prague spring is exhaustive, but in a way fragmented, and—besides a few exceptions—with each national historiography giving its soliloquy. Thus, it was high time to start an international dialogue and to investigate and analyse the reactions of the key international players and Warsaw pact member states involved in the invasion, to bring to the debate the newest findings of the respective national historiographies.

Jakub Drábik

02
Reflections on 1968 and its Legacies

Jacques Rupnik
Sciences Po, Paris

"Czechoslovakia in 1968 represented an important moment in human history; it did not represent an important international crisis."[1] The verdict of two eminent British professors of international relations, arrived at instantly after the tanks of August put an end to the Czechoslovak experiment of 'socialism with human face', was brutal and painfully accurate. The division of the continent was confirmed and a new version of east-west 'détente,' based on that understanding, ready to be launched. The significance of the Prague Spring cannot be measured only by its defeat, however. Its contribution should be understood in the interplay between its Czecho-Slovak and European dimensions. The August '68 invasion might not have provoked a "major international crisis," as the two professors stated, but it certainly was the year that shook Europe. Three aspects deserve to be mentioned in this respect. First, the Prague Spring revived the debate about Czechoslovak democratic exceptionalism in the context of (east) European Socialism. Second, it was often interpreted as part of an international, generational revolt against the establishments, east and west. Third, it represented the most far-reaching reform of the system within the Soviet sphere and provided twenty years later a belated (and thus doomed) inspiration for Mikhail Gorbachev's botched attempt to save it, which indeed paved the way for 1989.

The Prague Spring was not what you read about in school textbooks that start with the election of Alexander Dubček as party leader on January 5, 1968 and conclude with the Soviet-led invasion of August 21. Rather, it should be understood as a process starting in the early 1960s, with converging pressures for economic reforms identified with the name Ota Sik; Slovak resentment of Prague centralism (hence Alexander Dubček and the

---

[1] Philip Windsor and Adam Roberts, *Czechoslovakia, 1968: Reform, Repression, Resistance* (New York: Columbia University Press, 1969).

federalization project); and the gradual emancipation of the cultural sphere from the stranglehold of ideological censorship, which accounts for the golden age of Czech cinema, theater, and literature with a significant and lasting impact throughout Europe. The culmination of the three-pronged process brought about political change, starting with the abolition of censorship and the separation of party and state. In other words, 1968 was not just a parlor game for reform-minded party bureaucrats. It was, in Václav Havel's words, "above all a civic renewal, a restoration of human dignity, the trust in the capacities and possibilities of citizens to change society."[2]

Post-1968 interpretations of the democratization process revived variations on the theme of Czechoslovak exceptionalism in east central Europe. The first could be summed up as the triumph of Czech and Slovak culture over the Communist structure. The emancipation of the cultural sphere from the constraints of censorship without being subjected to market pressures produced a powerful 60s cultural background to the political and societal changes associated with 1968. A related version of the argument concerns the enduring democratic character of Czechoslovak political culture. Authors like Archie Brown and Gordon Skilling are instructive here. Skilling, in his monumental study of the Prague Spring, has argued that the legacies of pre-war democracy, followed between 1945 and 1948 by a "democratic interlude," have left behind a political culture (both broadly in society and specifically within the Communist Party itself) that were in conflict with the Stalinist regime, and that eventually came to the surface in the 1960s to contribute to a break from Soviet-type Communism.[3] Hence, the problematic title of Skilling's book, *The Interrupted Revolution*. In contrast to the Hungarian revolution of 1956, and in order to avoid a similar outcome, the Prague reformers were eager to stress that they meant change within socialism. Yet abolishing censorship and separating party and state fostered a dynamic that challenged the fundamentals of the Communist system.

---

2   Václav Havel, "La citoyenneté retrouvée," Introduction to J. Rupnik and F. Fejtö, eds., *Le printemps tchécoslovaque 1968* (Bruxelles: Editions Complexes, 1999), 12.
3   Gordon H. Skilling, *Czechoslovakia's Interrupted Revolution* (Princeton: Princeton University Press, 1976); Archie Brown and Gordon Wightman, "Czechoslovakia: Revival and Retreat," in Archie Brown and Jack Gray, eds., *Political Culture and Political Change in Communist States* (New York: Macmillan, 1977), 159–96.

One of the most interesting debates about the meaning of 1968 was expressed through the opposition of two leading Czech intellectuals, Milan Kundera and Václav Havel—a debate which is worth re-reading half a century later, although not for a post-invasion assessment.[4] Inspired by the formidable, peaceful civic resistance of August 1968, Kundera overstated the case when he said that the reformist project could survive the invasion, and this was mercilessly dismissed by Havel as sheer delusion. It is the meaning of the Spring of 1968, however, which is worth revisiting. Following on H. Gordon Schauer's provocative nineteenth century question about what ultimately justifies the efforts put into producing a culture in the Czech language, Kundera makes a plea for the contribution of small nations to universal values, ideas, culture:

> A small nation, if it has any meaning in the world, has to daily, constantly re-create itself. The moment it ceases to create values, it loses the justification for its existence and then perhaps actually ceases to exist, because it is fragile and vulnerable. The creation of values is connected with its very being.[5]

For Kundera, the Prague Spring was of significance to Europe as a whole because, beyond eastern Stalinism and western Capitalism, it tried to combine Socialism with democracy. Not a mere remake of the 'third way', nor a blueprint for a radiant future, the Czechoslovak heresy was defeated, but its impact on the future of the European Left has been far-reaching and persistent.

Havel's take, in contrast, was more sober and realistic, far from the 'provincial messianism' he attributed to Kundera. Restoring basic freedoms was no doubt a great achievement, but the last time we had them was thirty years ago and indeed this is considered 'normal' in most 'civilized' countries. Therefore, 1968 was about liberal democratic normality, as opposed to the repressive 'normalization' that followed:

> ... If we are going to imagine that a country has placed itself at the center of world history because it wishes to establish freedom of expression—something taken for granted in most of the civilized world—and to check the tyranny of its secret police, in all seriousness we shall become nothing more than self-complacent hacks,

---

4   Milan Kundera, "Český úděl," *Literarni Listy* 7–8, December 19, 1968, ("Czech Destiny"), trans. Tim West; Václav Havel, "Český úděl?" ("Czech Destiny"), *Tvar*, April 1969. The three articles (with Kundera's reply to Havel) reprinted in *Literarni Noviny*, December 27, 2007.
5   Milan Kundera, "Český úděl," 5.

laughable in our provincial messianism! Freedom and the rule of law are the most basic preconditions for a normally and soundly functioning societal organism, and should any state attempt to reestablish them after years of their absence it is doing nothing historically momentous but simply trying to remove its own abnormality.[6]

For some thirty years the verdict on Kundera's somewhat messianic vision vs Havel's lucid realism seemed fairly obvious to most Czechs. Yet today, half a century later, with Communism long dead and western liberal-democratic 'normalcy' in crisis, Kundera's plea for the 'Czechoslovak possibility' in 1968 acquires perhaps a new resonance.

A second reading of the Prague Spring highlights its European dimension and calls us to interpret it through the prism of the rebellions that shook the political establishments throughout the continent in '68. There was May '68 in France, the Polish events of March '68, Berlin, Belgrade ...

The common denominator of these movements was the search for alternative models of society with contrasting, confusing, and often contradictory references to 'Socialism': from self-management in the workplace to the Christian-Marxist dialogue or to discussions about the impact of science and technology on the evolution of modern societies in both east and west. Moreover, there were not insignificant Czech contributions to all of the above. Karel Kosik's Marxist humanism (influenced by Jan Patocka's phenomenology) and a civilizational pessimism related precisely to the dehumanizing role of science and technology, or on the contrary, Radovan Richta's civilizational optimism based on the "scientific and technical revolution."[7] The former proved incompatible with the "normalization" *Gleichschaltung* of the 1970s, while the latter's technocratic faith in the progress of sciences rather easily blended in. Both were among the most influential Czech thinkers of the late 1960s in Europe and both were thus part of what Jan Patocka had in mind in attempting to frame the Prague Spring reforms in a European context and calling for a dialogue between intellectuals east and west. Patocka's contribution was a piece entitled "Inteligence a opozice," based on a lecture given during the Spring of 1968 in Germany, where he states that "the position of intellectuals in the

---

6   Václav Havel, Český úděl?
7   1968 was the year Karel Kosik's *Dialectic of the Concrete* (Dialektika konkrétniho, 1966) and Radovan Richta's *Civilization at the Crossroads* (Civilizace na rozcesti, 1967) were translated in western Europe.

East is better because 'they do not consider basic democratic rights as a mere means towards an end but an end in itself'."[8]

This proved to be the main contrast between 1968 in Prague (or Warsaw) and Paris (or Berlin). To be sure, there is a whole aspect of 1968 that can be interpreted mainly in terms of generations. There is now even a term for this: "Youthquake," declared in 2017 as the "Word of the Year" by the experts at the Oxford English Dictionary. It is defined as "significant cultural, political, or social change arising from the actions or influence of young people." The most interesting thing about the Prague Spring was that there was indeed youth participation, particularly the student movement as its radical wing, but its driving force was the previous generation, which experienced (supported or was at the receiving end of) state actions in 1945–48 and their aftermath. A.J. Liehm, the editor of *Literarni listy* in 1968, elaborated on this concept of political generations precisely in 1968 in the introduction to a splendid volume of his interviews with the leading intellectual figures of 1968 (from Ludvik Vaculik to Josef Skvorecky, and from Eduard Goldstücker to Václav Havel, to mention only a few), among the best guides to the cultural politics of the Prague Spring.[9] Many—by no means all—of those who turned twenty after World War Two and had backed the communist takeover in 1948 found themselves frustrated and disappointed with the revolution from above, and thus helped in the 1960s to bring about a revolution from below, which culminated in 1968.[10]

As much as the political context, this generational aspect accounts for the contrasts and misunderstandings of 1968 between east and west, Prague and Paris. The driving force of the Prague Spring was the aspiration to freedom, whereas in Paris the moment of emancipation combined with the myth of revolution. Milan Kundera described the contrast as follows:

---

8   Jan Patocka, *Sebrané Spisy*, vol. 12 (Prague: OIKOYMENH, 2016), 241–43.
9   Antonin J. Liehm, "Generace znamena v cestine singular i plural," Introduction to *Generace* (Praha, 1969 [banned before distribution] and 1990). The book was translated in several languages with a lengthy afterword by Jean-Paul Sartre, "The Socialism that Came in from the Cold," Introduction to Antonin J. Liehm, *The Politics of Culture* (New York: Grove, 1973).
10 Their radicalism in undoing what they had helped to bring about two decades earlier perplexed the non-communists and particularly those belonging to an in-between generational group: see the samizdat volume *Zivot je vsude, Almanach roku 1956* (Praha: Paseka, 2005), edited by Josef Hiršal and Jiří Kolář, with contributions of Skvorecky, Hrabal, Julis, Kolar, Hirsal, Zabrana, Kubena and a certain Václav Havel.

> Paris's May '68 was an explosion of revolutionary lyricism. The Prague Spring was the explosion of post-revolutionary skepticism ... May '68 was a radical uprising whereas what had, for many a long year, been leading towards the explosion of the Prague Spring was a popular revolt by moderates.[11]

While western radicals beset by post-colonial guilt looked to the Third World, European identity was part of the Spring of 1968 in Prague. Again, in Kundera's words:

> Paris in May '68 challenged the basis of what is called European culture and its traditional values. The Prague Spring was a passionate defense of the European cultural tradition in the widest and most tolerant sense of the term (a defense of Christianity just as much as of modern art—both rejected by those in power). We all struggled for the right to maintain that tradition that had been threatened by the anti-western messianism of Russian totalitarianism."[12]

The contrast and misunderstandings highlighted here, however, should not make us forget the intellectually and politically important convergence between the western '68ers who in the following decade abandoned Marxism and became anti-totalitarian liberals of different shades, and the post-'68 Czech dissidents around common issues and concerns: human rights, civil society, and overcoming the partition of Europe.

Finally, there is another dimension to the Spring of 1968 as the "supreme stage" of reformism in the Soviet bloc and its implications for a divided Europe. Zdenek Mlynar, one of the architects of the political reforms and in 1968 the youngest member of the Politburo, has described the way Leonid Brezhnev and the Soviet leadership spelled out the reasons for the invasion to Dubček and his colleagues:

> Precisely because the territorial results of the last war are untouchable to us we had to intervene in Czechoslovakia. The West will not move, so, what do you think will be done on your behalf? Comrades Tito, Ceausescu, Berlinguer, will make speeches. Well, and what of it? You are counting on the Communist movement in Western Europe? But that has remained insignificant for the last fifty years.[13]

---

11 Milan Kundera, Preface to the French edition of Josef Skvorecky and Claudia Ancelot, *Miracle en Bohème* [*Mirákl: Politická detektivka* in original Czech] (Paris: Gallimard, 1978), x.
12 Ibid., x–xi.
13 Zdenek Mlynar, *Mraz prichazi z Kremlu* (Köln: Index, 1979), 306–7. Translated into English as *Nightfrost in Prague: The End of Humane Socialism* (New York: Karz Publishers, 1980).

That part is familiar enough. Indeed Tito and the "Eurocommunists" in the west protested and claimed to continue the legacy of the Prague Spring as a way to enhance their democratic credentials in western Europe.

The real legacy, however, returned with a vengeance twenty years later. Gorbachev, Mlynar's friend and roommate from their student days in Moscow, became leader of the Soviet Communist Party and sought inspiration for his perestroika in the Prague Spring of 1968. Asked what was the difference between his reforms and those of Dubček, the spokesman for Gorbachev replied simply: "Nineteen years" …

That certainly was not good enough to rehabilitate "socialism with a human face" in the eyes of skeptical Czechs and Slovaks twenty years later. It is not easy to identify with a defeated project that carries the price tag of another twenty years in a post-totalitarian dictatorship. It did matter, however, for what was unfolding in Moscow and its relationship with its most western dependencies. Jiří Dienstbier, a prominent Czech journalist from 1968 and a dissident turned prisoner turned stoker, became Minister of foreign affairs in December 1989. On his first meeting with Gorbachev, he referred to the hopes of 1968 and their crushing by Moscow, to which Gorbachev replied: "We thought that we had strangled the Prague Spring while in reality we had strangled ourselves …"[14]

Gorbachev and his entourage saw the Prague Spring as a chance to save the system. Its crushing thus prevented reform at the very center of the empire and accounts for its delayed but intractable crisis. In other words, the August 1968 invasion, by preventing structural change in Czechoslovakia, prepared the ground for the unraveling of "actually existing socialism" (Brezhnev dixit). To be sure, there is tough competition for the title of "who contributed most" to the demise of the Soviet empire. The Hungarians point to the revolution of 1956, the Poles see Solidarity (*Solidarność*) in 1980, the largest social movement in post-war Europe, which, despite being put down by Jaruzelski's military coup, was the swan song of the communist regime. The contribution of the Prague Spring of 1968, even crushed violently, should not be underestimated.

Appropriately, for a major Czechoslovak crisis in the twentieth century, the 'Velvet Revolution' of 1989 came late. It had initially been

---

14 J. Dienstbier, quoted in G.E. Castellano and D. Jun, "The Awkward Revolution," *The New Presence* (Winter 2008): 17.

planned for 1988. Gorbachev's procrastination and other circumstances probably account for the minor delay that put the Velvet Revolution among the fateful eights of the country's history.[15] It should be noted, however, that although it was obviously understood as the undoing of the legacy of the 1948 communist takeover, it was not framed as a continuation of the "interrupted revolution" of 1968. To be sure, some sidelined 68ers and a number of western observers were inclined to point to that continuity with the aspirations of the Prague Spring, but the main protagonists of 1989 in Prague were eager to distance themselves from the "illusions of 1968." The aim was no longer the democratization of socialism but simply democracy. Instead of searching for a 'third way' between capitalism and Soviet-style Socialism, the goal was the introduction of markets without adjectives: "the third way leads to the Third World" said Václav Klaus, the promoter of radical free-market economic reforms. Furthermore, the "return to Europe," translated into foreign policy terms, was no longer about extending the margins of maneuvering in central Europe between east and west, but to join western ("Euro-Atlantic") institutions as quickly as possible. Václav Havel rather than Alexander Dubček became president and the embodiment of these goals.

The reasons are understandable: it was not easy in 1989 to identify with a project that crashed tragically and was followed by twenty years of relentless 'normalization.' In dealing with the divide between '68ers and '89ers, it may be useful to distinguish between "illusions" (ideas that you can reform the system from within the Communist Party) and utopias (which entail a future-oriented project known as 'socialism with a human face'). All one can add is that 1968 was the last Czech attempt to propose not a blueprint but a vision (deemed utopian or inconsistent afterwards), which transcended the country and concerned Europe as a whole. By way of contrast, 1989 was the first revolution not to propose a new social project; a revolution without violence and utopias, but also without a strong new idea. It was indeed, as historian François Furet called it, a "revolution-restoration" or, as Jürgen Habermas called it, "catch-up revolution"

---

15   The national independence and formation of the Czechoslovak Republic in 1918, the Munich Agreement of 1938, the seizing of complete power by the Communist Party in 1948, 1968 and the 'Velvet Revolution' of 1988/89.

(*Nachholende Revolution*).¹⁶ The aim was to restore national and popular sovereignty, the rule of law, private property, and to imitate the western model. For that reason, the Velvet Revolution of 1989 has since the 1990s been considered in Prague as an "anti-1968," and today the commemorations concern the tragedy of the invasion of August 1968 rather than the hopes and aspirations of the Spring.

Understandable as the distancing from the ideas and illusions of 1968 may be, it has, two potential snags: if your aim is to imitate western economic and political models, you cease to be interesting for the west. In addition, and more importantly, what if you are imitating a model in crisis? In thinking that one through, you may be forgiven for straying and stumbling upon ideas, projects, and utopias associated with the Prague Spring of 1968.

---

16 See for example, François Furet, *L'Enigme de la désagrégation communiste* (Paris: Fondation Saint Simon, 1990); and Jürgen Habermas, *Die nachholende Revolution: Kleine Plotisiche Schriften VII* (Frankfurt: Suhrkamp Verlag, 1990): 179–94.

03
The Prague Spring and the Evolution of the Position of Leonid Brezhnev

Alexander Stykalin
Institute of Slavic Studies, Russian Academy of Sciences, Moscow

The reforms of 1968 in Czechoslovakia, stopped by the August 21 intervention, continue to attract attention of historians in Russia, as we can see from the considerable number of documentary publications as well as scholarly studies based on archives research.[17] The published documents reveal the dynamics of the view of the Soviet leadership towards the internal processes in Czechoslovakia, the measures taken to disturb the reforms (especially the reforms of political structure which threatened the monopoly of the Communist Part), the preparation for military action, its propaganda and political support, as well as the response of intellectuals and wider circles of the Soviet society on the intervention.[18] The documents

---

17 The most important volume of studies in Russian is: 1968 год. "Пражская весна". Историческая ретроспектива [1968. The Prague Spring. The Historical Retrospective]. Москва (M.), 2010. The book is based on the reports of the large-scale international conference held in October 2008, the studies touch the main aspects of the subject and especially the Soviet-Czechoslovak relations at the high level, the activities of the Soviet Embassy, the international context of the intervention, the reaction of the Western communist movement, the response of the Soviet public and especially of the intellectuals. The view of the official Moscow on the problem of Czechoslovak federalism and the settlement of relations between Prague and Slovakia was also reflected in the volume.

18 See the collections of documents: "Пражская весна" и международный кризис 1968 года. Документы [The Prague Spring and the International Crisis of 1968 in Czechoslovakia. Documents] M., 2010; Чехословацкий кризис 1967–1969 годов в документах ЦК КПСС [The Crisis of 1967–1969 in Czechoslovakia in the documents of the Central Committee of the Soviet Union]. M., 2010. These publications are based first of all on the documents of the Russian State Archive of Contemporary History (RGANI), former Archive of the Central Committee of the Soviet Communist Party. The first of these projects was realized by RGANI and Ludwig Boltzmann-Institut für Kriegsfolgen-Forschung (Graz, Austria), headed by Stefan Karner. The other joint project was realized by RGANI in cooperation with the Czech colleagues. The volumes contain some hundreds of documents—the records of the meetings of the Soviet and Eastern-European Communist leaders where the situation in Czechoslovakia was discussed

provide a more complete picture of the position of the Soviet political elite concerning all the sides of the development in Czechoslovakia, including the settlement of relations between Prague and Slovakia[19]. The documents let us see whether there was complete unity in the highest Soviet leadership on the use of force in Czechoslovakia, or there were some differences in the positions of individual representatives of the Soviet elite.

According to various sources, Kremlin anxieties at the situation in Czechoslovakia—including worries about Czech ideological and cultural policy Soviet leaders deemed too liberal—was manifested a few years before the Prague Spring. In 1966, Leonid Brezhnev visited the 13th Congress of the Communist Party of Czechoslovakia and, returning to Moscow, shared his impressions with his comrades at the meeting of party activists. He expressed displeasure with too sharp criticism in the speeches of some speakers at Prague's Congress. "Here in Moscow we need to protect ourselves from such things", he noted.[20]

Nevertheless, there was not too much anxiety, and if anybody who visited Czechoslovakia tried to sound such an alarm, it was not supported. One Komsomol functionary, who visited Czechoslovakia in 1964, wrote in his report that the Communist Party had completely lost its influence over Czechoslovak youth, who took their lead now from Western values. As the result he was accused of spreading slander and attempting to undermine the Czech-Soviet youth relations. The case was closed and he was not expelled from the Communist party only because his information about the weakening of party control over the youth in Czechoslovakia was confirmed from other influential sources[21].

---

since March 1968, the interparty correspondence, the reports of the Soviet Embassy in Prague, the instructions for the internal party organizations aimed at the explanation of the Soviet policy at a lower level of the Soviet Communist Party.

19 We refer here first of all to the records of the sessions of the Politburo of the Soviet Communist Party, of the Soviet-Czechoslovakian high-level talks and of the summits of the leaders of the Soviet and Eastern-European Communist Parties.

20 Testimony of the well-known Russian journalist Alexander Bovin, who in the 1960s was a speechwriter for Brezhnev: Бовин А. XX век как жизнь [XX century as a life]. М., 2003. С. 175.

21 На идеологическом посту: 1960-е. Воспоминания сотрудников ЦК КПСС [On the ideological post: 1960s. Memories of the functionaries of the CPSU Central Committee] // Неприкосновенный запас. Дебаты о политике и культуре. М., 2008. № 4. С. 154–158.

Soviet leaders were well informed of the increasingly active demands by Slovak people for reform—and of the need for decentralization (felt and expressed by party members too), The sharp criticism of Antonín Novotný by Alexander Dubček in the fall of 1967 was no of secret in Moscow especially since Dubček on his own initiative had contacts with Soviet journalists and made them clear his position both on the Slovak question and the necessary reforms in the whole country[22]. In December 1967, when Brezhnev himself went to Prague to see with his own eyes and to assess the state of affairs, the question of the relationship between the center and Slovakia seemed to him one of the priorities in terms of stability in the country[23].

It is known that on the eve of the final session of the plenum of the Czechoslovak Communist Party, where in early January 1968 Novotný's successor was chosen, Dubček's candidacy as the first secretary of the Communist Party did not raise opposition of the official Moscow[24]. In childhood, he lived a long time in the USSR, he was a veteran of the Czechoslovak Communist Party, had long-standing and close ties with Soviet party functionaries and was not considered to be a politically unpredictable person. He was known as one of Antonín Novotný's active opponents but Novotný was not perceived at that time to be a guarantee of stability and his support as the party leader has long ceased to be an axiom for Moscow. Brezhnev, during his conversations with high-ranking Czechoslovak Communists, qualified the question of re-electing the party's first secretary as an internal Czechoslovak affair.[25]

This made the subsequent disappointment in Dubček all the stronger. Moscow's anxiety over the course of events in Czechoslovakia was manifested later, in March, under the influence of information received from the Soviet Embassy. The weakening of censorship and the resignation of many functionaries who were considered to be reliable partners

---

22   See the testimony of V. Krivosheev who was the correspondent of "Izvestiya" in Prague in 1965–1968: Вторжение: Взгляд из России. Чехословакия, август 1968 [Intervention: the view from Russia. Czechoslovakia, august 1968]/Составитель Й. Паздерка. М., 2016. С. 131–138.
23   Brezhnev visited Prague on December 8, 1967. See: Латыш М.В. "Пражская весна" 1968 г. и реакция Кремля [The Prague Spring of 1968 and the reaction of the Kremlin]. М., 1998. С. 17–18.
24   See about the reaction of the Soviet Embassy on the election of Dubček as the first secretary of the Party: Ibid., p. 23.
25   Ibid., p. 18.

of Moscow caused the greatest concern in the Kremlin, where they were afraid not only to lose control over Czechoslovakia but that the Czeh and Slovak reformers would set an example to those elsewhere in the USSR who were tempted by the prospect of liberalizing the Soviet system. It is well-known however that on March 23rd in Dresden (Eastern Germany), where the first meeting of the Soviet and East-European Communist Party leaders was held to assess the situation in Czechoslovakia, Brezhnev's speeches were much more calm and moderate than Walter Ulbricht's and Władysław Gomułka's. This is confirmed by some lesser known sources, including the notes of the leader of the Ukrainian Soviet Communist Party organization in 1968 Petro Shelest, one of the main hawks in the Soviet leadership, who took part in Dresden talks as a member of the CPSU delegation. Shelest in his notes strongly criticized Brezhnev's position (including that on the Dresden talks) as not too resolute and irreconcilable[26]. If we would try to explain the roots of his position, it must be taken into account the KGB information from Eastern Slovakia concerning some attempts to revitalize the Greece-Catholic Church[27]—that was the principal question for Western Ukraine where this Church was one of the foundation stones of Ukrainian anti-communist national movement. The Ukrainian Communist elite feared that impulses from Czechoslovakia, especially from Slovakia, will provoke national trends in Western Ukraine.

It is known that in early April the Action Program of the Communist Party of Czechoslovakia was adopted—the main conceptual document that brought the views of the Prague Communist reformers into system. The reaction in Moscow was quite negative. The document was qualified as the challenge to the indisputable right of the CPSU to form the guidelines of the Communist movement and the basic concepts of Socialism. It is precisely after the publication of the Action Program that Moscow's view on the reform process in Czechoslovakia became tougher—the program of the Czechoslovakian reformers was criticized at the April Party plenum of

---

[26] See: Шелест П.Е. Да не судимы будете: Дневниковые записи, воспоминания члена Политбюро ЦК КПСС. [Let not be judged. The Notes of Diaries, the Memories of the member of the Politbiuro CC CPSU]. М., 1995. С. 301.

[27] 30 Октября [October 30] (издание общества "Международный Мемориал"). М., 2008. № 89. История инакомыслия. С. 7.

the Central Committee CPSU[28], the campaign of criticism in the central Soviet press of the entire reform process in Czechoslovakia was launched at that time. According to some sources as early as in April the Soviet military headquarters intensified the working out of concrete plans for military action in Czechoslovakia in case the political leadership would prefer the force variant of actions to stop "revisionist" trends. It is known from the memoirs of general A. Maiorov who was in 1968 the commander of the Karpatian military district that as early as in middle-April the instructions were got how to act in the case of the preparation of the military operation[29]. On April 8, 1968, the commander of the airborne troops, General V. Margelov, according to the directive received, began to elaborate the plan of using airborne forces in Czechoslovakia[30].

On April 28, 1968 the Yugoslavian leader Iosip Broz Tito came to Moscow after a long tour of the Asian countries and the next day had a long conversation with Brezhnev. The situation in Czechoslovakia became the main subject of discussion between leaders of the two countries[31]. The Soviet side hoped for the proximity of the Soviet and Yugoslav viewpoints, bearing in mind that relations between the USSR and Yugoslavia had been improving since 1965—Yugoslavia supported the Soviet view on the middle-Eastern crisis of June 1967 (the six day war between Izrael and three Arabian countries) and in November Tito visited Moscow and took part in the celebrations of the 50th anniversary of the Bolsheviks' revolution. Moscow attached importance to the Yugoslav view on the reform processes in Czechoslovakia, taking into account the international prestige of

---

28   On April 10, Brezhnev spoke at the plenum with the report "On the actual problems of the international situation and the CPSU's struggle for the unity of the world communist movement", which was not fully published in the Soviet press in order to avoid aggravating the Soviet-Chinese controversy. The report also criticized the Czechoslovak Communists for their concessions to revisionism and the weakening of the role of the ruling party.

29   Майоров А. Вторжение. Чехословакия 1968. Свидетельства командарма [Intervention. Czechoslovakia 1968, The Testimonies of the Commander of the Army]. М., 1998. С. 19–21.

30   Кыров А. Десантники в операции "Дунай" (Советско-чехословацкие военно-политические отношения, 1968 [Paratroopers in Operation Danube (Soviet-Czechoslovak military-political relations, 1968]. М., 1996.

31   Встречи и переговоры на высшем уровне руководителей СССР и Югославии в 1946–1980 гг. [Meetings and negotiations at the highest level of the leaders of the USSR and Yugoslavia in 1946–1980] Том второй. 1965–1980. М., 2017. С. 211–230.

Tito as not only one of the founders and leaders of non-alignment movement, but as a person who at one time had the courage to challenge Stalin. Brezhnev did not hide from the Yugoslav leader his concern about the weakening of the CPCz leadership's control over the political processes in the country, and at that time, for 4 months before the intervention, frankly expressed his opinion. In many respects, that opinion corresponded to the so-called Brezhnev doctrine (the doctrine of limited sovereignty), formulated later in the Declaration of Communist Parties in Bratislava in early August 1968 and—especially—in a number of the Soviet program declarations, 'Pravda' articles and the speeches by Soviet leaders after August 21. On April 29, 1968, during the talks with Tito, Brezhnev noted:

> We need some radical steps on our part in order to help Czechoslovakia stand on the positions of socialism. Do not be afraid of the word 'intervention'. After all, we are proletarian internationalists and we are not indifferent to the fate of socialism in other countries. There are issues that can not be regarded as purely Soviet or purely Yugoslav. We have common tasks and responsibilities arising from the principles of proletarian internationalism. We are very concerned and we are not indifferent to how our friends are doing, including in Yugoslavia, 'where economic reform,' in comradely terms, it seems to us, has not yet yielded positive results.[32]

In such remarks, Tito could see the exposition of the program, which posed a challenge not only for Czechoslovakia, but also for Yugoslavia. For his part, the Yugoslavian leader made some critical remarks on the policy of Dubček and his team, but at the same time made it clear that he supported the current Czechoslovak leadership, suggesting that, if assisted, it could cope with the situation. Thus, the Soviet leaders had to take note that any military or otherwise coercive action against Czechoslovakia would hardly find the support of the Yugoslav side. The negative reaction of Titoist Yugoslavia as well as of the national-Communist Romania on the August Intervention is well known. Recently published documents give us some new details. His extremely negative attitude to the intervention (which dealt in his opinion a severe blow to the idea of Socialism on the international level), Tito expounded to the Soviet ambassador Ivan Benediktov, whom he received on August 31. As for Yugoslavia, Tito made it clear to the ambassador that the Yugoslavs themselves solve their problems and will not allow anyone from outside to interfere in their affairs. If anybody threatens, it does not matter from the West or from the East,

---

32 Ibid., p. 223–224.

"Yugoslavia,—as Tito put it,—will fight resolutely, defending its independence. This can not be doubted".[33]

Some months later this line changed to some extent. The next meeting with Benediktov Tito held on October 19. By this time, under pressure of Moscow an agreement on the temporary stay of Soviet troops in Czechoslovakia had already been signed (following the results of the bilateral Soviet-Czechoslovak summit meeting held on October 3–4, 1968). This somewhat calmed the Yugoslav leader, who apparently decided to stop raising the Czechoslovak question. Tito told the Soviet ambassador: "Goodwill is important now. I said today that I see no reason that every day in our newspapers be written about Czechoslovakia. In Moscow, an agreement was signed. We would not want to interfere in its implementation".[34] And on September 4, 1969 (already after considerable personnel changes in the party-state apparatus, the removal of many reformers from responsible positions) Tito, receiving the Minister of Foreign Affairs of the USSR Andrei Gromyko developed his position. He confirmed his and the entire Yugoslav leadership's view that the military invasion caused "great damage both to socialism in Czechoslovakia and to socialism in general". "We spoke", he continued, "we took our principled position on the events in Czechoslovakia and we do not back down from it. But at the same time, we considered that the situation around Czechoslovakia should not be dramatized, and we were able to minimize publications in our press. In the end, we cannot be more Czech than the Czechs. Let the Czechs and Slovaks themselves decide this question. And with Czechoslovakia, despite the fact who is now in power, we seek good relations".[35] By the autumn of 1971, when the first meeting between Brezhnev and Tito after a 3-year interval took place, the disagreements on the Czechoslovak issue were not more a factor which seriously affected the Soviet-Yugoslav relations.

In May 1968, Prime Minister Alexei Kosygin visited Czechoslovakia, he met with many members of the Communist elite and came to the conclusion that the positions of those whom Moscow considered to be some kind of alternative to the reform line of Dubček's team were very weak. The idea of conducting military maneuvers on the territory of

---

33   Ibid., p. 236.
34   Ibid., p. 243.
35   Ibid., p. 263.

Czechoslovakia in order to exert forceful pressure on its leadership was not abandoned (the maneuvers took place in late June). At the same time, the decision was made to influence Dubček and his team, in order to correct their course, which was considered in Moscow to be unacceptable. In June such kind of line was dominant in Moscow. It was reassessed only in the end of June after the publication on June 27 of the program document of the Czech non-communist intellectual opposition "2000 thousand words", written by Ludvík Vaculík This document was perceived by the Soviets as a sign that the communist leadership in Czechoslovakia had absolutely lost the control over the situation, the non-Communist opposition had seized the initiative in developing a reform program, and this created a real threat to the Communist monopoly on power[36].

In July, the leaders of the USSR prepared military action—covering all details, including propaganda. The declarations of the new Czechoslovak government were worked out and approved at the Politburo session on July 26–27,[37] but the Soviets also gave Dubček's team the last chance to "improve" the situation according their expectations. As is known well, new attempts to exert pressure on him were made in late July during bilateral talks at Čierna nad Tisou and in early August at a multiparty summit in Bratislava (the final declaration, which anticipated some of the theses later at the core of the Brezhnev doctrine)[38].

The views of all the members of the Soviet leadership can be reconstructed on the basis of records of their notes both at meetings of the Soviet

---

[36] We can also note that it was precisely after the publication of the '2000 words' that the position of the Hungarian leadership, and in particular of János Kádár, who so far generally supported the economic component of the Czechoslovak reforms, became noticeably tougher. This follows both from public speeches by Kádár, including that he made during his visit to Moscow in early July, and from his position, outlined at his talks with Dubček, not long before the Warsaw meeting of leaders of the Communist Parties which took place in middle June (the Czechoslovak delegation did not come to Warsaw. Despite the increasing convergence of positions of Brezhnev and Kádár it was Kádár who tried to persuade the communist leadership of Czechoslovakia to seek a compromise demonstrating to Moscow the desire to take measures against non-communist opposition, but Kádár's mission was not successful (see in this volume the study of Miklós Mitrovics).

[37] See the materials: Чехословацкий кризис 1967–1969 годов в документах ЦК КПСС.

[38] See: Суверенитет и интернациональные обязанности социалистических стран [Sovereignty and international obligations of socialist countries] // Правда, 1968, 26 сентября.

Politburo and during bilateral talks at Čierna nad Tisou.[39] Without exception, all were sure that it was necessary to put an end to the reform processes in Czechoslovakia, since they were leading to a weakening of the monopoly power of the Communist elite. However, there were some differences in assessing the methods of action. This was manifested, for example, in a clash at a Politburo meeting by the more moderate Kosygin with a more radical Yurii Andropov, KGB chief. Andropov was at that time only a candidate member of the Politburo, but the comrades paid special attention to his opinion because they knew that he had a real experience in Hungary as the Soviet ambassador during the 1956 revolution[40]. Andropov often turned to the experience of the Hungarian events, trying to draw parallels with what was happening in Czechoslovakia. He used to remind his colleagues that the so-called "counterrevolution" was preceded by a lengthy ideological preparation led by writers, journalists, intellectuals[41].

As for Brezhnev, caution and indecisiveness were fully manifested in all his activities before intervention. On the one hand, he knew very well that if Communist power in Czechoslovakia were to weaken and the political system and economic model were to be reformed and become less like Soviet models, his party comrades would use it against him as the party leader. His position at the head of the party was not yet sufficiently strong in 1968 and the weakening of Soviet influence in Czechoslovakia could be used by his rivals as an occasion for removing him from office, as well as Khruschev just four years before. On the other hand, Brezhnev for a long time did not see in Czechoslovakia any strong and influential alternative to Dubček's team which would be realistically supported by Moscow. Gustáv Husák was supported as the candidate for the top position in the

---

39 The first study where the subject was deeply examined is: Латыш М.В. "Пражская весна" 1968 г. и реакция Кремля.

40 For more on his position and his activities in Hungary of 1956, see: Советский дипломат перед национал-коммунистическим вызовом. Ю.В. Андропов в Венгрии (1953–1957) [Soviet diplomat in front of the national communist challenge. Yu.V. Andropov in Hungary (1953–1957)] // Стыкалин А.С. Венгерский кризис 1956 года в исторической ретроспективе. М., 2016. С. 33–78.

41 See in detail: Стыкалин А.С. Память о венгерских событиях 1956 г. в период Пражской весны 1968 г. [The memory of the Hungarian events of 1956 in the period of the Prague Spring of 1968] // Социальные последствия войн и конфликтов XX века: историческая память. М.–Спб., "Нестор", 2014. С. 279–287.

party only after August 21 when—after the examining other candidates—Moscow came to the conclusion that they were even weaker and unacceptable for various reasons (not least their unpopularity, the lack of minimal support from below). We can also deduce that in the Kremlin they could realize that it was possible to make more active use of Slovak nationalism against the Prague reformers, and that this was an important argument in favor of Husák.

When in July 1968 the Soviets started to prepare the decisive forceful action, the naturally cautious Brezhnev showed repeatedly at Politburo meetings his concern about the fact that poorly prepared intervention could only complicate the situation. Even in August, after the Bratislava summit, he exerted considerable effort (during telephone conversations) to influence Dubček in order to take control of the media, to limit the public activity of intellectuals and replace the most unacceptable for Moscow members of his team, including František Kriegel. Brezhnev's hesitation was a factor slowing to some extent the decision-making on military intervention. Thus, on July 19 he exclaimed at the session of the Politburo: have we exhausted all the means from the arsenal of political influence; have we done everything to avoid the extreme measures?[42] The delay over a military solution which might take place as early as in late July, just after the summit in Warsaw (July 14–15), was not the result of any polemics in the Soviet leadership, but primarily the internal doubts from Brezhnev himself, who by 1968 had become the first number in the country's leadership and used the opportunity to demonstrate to his comrades his political will and weight. Prone to hesitation, he was inclined to take extreme measures only under the pressure of immutable circumstances.

Brezhnev made his final choice when it became clear to him that he had not succeeded in persuading the Czechoslovak side to reject the idea of holding the extraordinary party congress where, as it was expected, would be made decisive personnel changes.

As early as on August 21 they realized in Moscow that the plan to lead the new government to power had failed and it would be necessary to resume negotiations with the acting political team. Famously, Dubček's

---

[42] Пихоя Р.Г. Чехословакия, 1968. Взгляд из Москвы. По документам ЦК КПСС [Czechoslovakia, 1968. View from Moscow. According to documents of the Central Committee of the CPSU] // Новая и новейшая история, 1995. № 1. С. 35.

team, in its desire to avoid bloodshed, went on a far-reaching compromise with Moscow. Brezhnev from his side clearly feared a lot of bloodshed, which can cause new complications. It was just his initiative to send to Prague on the eve of the intervention Kirill Mazurov: one of the members of Politburo should leave for Prague for control the whole operation, otherwise the generals would act too rudely. It is known also that during long discussions on Czechoslovak issue on August 20 Berzhnev expressed his principal view that the borders would be opened: if anticommunists and "counter-revolutionaries" would prefer to leave the country, the Soviets would welcome. Otherwise, they would have to intern too many people and would not know what to do with them—a problem that indeed never existed for Stalin. Brezhnev's caution and indecision made it possible to prevent additional troubles that could occur due to the low level of political culture and to the political mood of the Soviet communist elite of that time.

Today, from the historical distance of 50 years we try to define the processes that took place in Czechoslovakia in 1968 and to reveal their main content. But even if we now read the attempts by Dubček and his associates to create socialism with a human face as utopian, we must nevertheless recognize that these people were motivated by sincere and noble intentions. The task of giving the existing system a more human face will never lose its relevance, even with respect to the most sophisticated political systems.

04
Limits of Washington's Position Towards the Invasion of Czechoslovakia in the Summer of 1968

Slavomír Michálek
Institute of History, Slovak Academy of Sciences, Bratislava

In the evening hours of the 20th of August 1968, the Soviet Ambassador to Washington, Anatoly F. Dobrynin visited the President of the USA Lyndon B. Johnson. State Secretary Dean Rusk was also present during the meeting.[43] The Ambassador Dobrynin claimed to have urgent instructions from his government to inform the president on an extremely serious issue:

> The government of the Soviet Union considers necessary to inform president Johnson in person ... in relation with further worsening of the situation caused by conspiracies of external powers of aggression against the existing social establishment in Czechoslovakia and against the statehood established by the constitution of this country, Czechoslovak government requested its allies, among them the Soviet Union, for direct help, military power included. The Soviet government repeatedly stresses the fact that the events in Czechoslovakia and around it are of vital importance to the Soviet Union and to the other countries bound by contractual obligations and that, the threat for the socialist order in Czechoslovakia creates at the same time a threat for the peace in Europe and security in the world. Therefore, the Soviet government and the governments of the allied countries have adopted a joint decision to fulfil the request of the Czechoslovak government who asked for indispensable help for the people of Czechoslovakia. Competent Soviet troops received the order to enter Czechoslovakia. Naturally, they will be immediately withdrawn as soon as the threat on security ends and we come to the conclusion their presence is no longer necessary. We want President Johnson to know that our steps, performed on basis of the request of the Czechoslovak government, are completely in accordance with the idea of strengthening the peace and under no circumstances an intention of threat for the state interests of the USA or other countries. We consider these events will not damage the Soviet-American relations, the Soviet government believes their development is, like in the past, of great importance.[44]

---

43   The study presented is a partial result of the project n. APVV-15-0349 "Indivíduum a spoločnosť—ich vzájomná reflexia v historickom procese," of the Institute of History of the Slovak Academy of Sciences/SAV.

44   Foreign Relations of the United States (further FRUS) 1964–1968, Volume XVII, Eastern Europe, Summary of meeting, Washington DC, August 20, 1968, 8:15–8:42 p.m.,

President Johnson thanked Dobrynin for the information and informed him he would consult Dean Rusk and—if he considered it appropriate—give him his answer. After a while, he unexpectedly changed the subject of the conversation and focused on his journey to the USSR. The end of the conversation was held in an almost free and friendly atmosphere, whisky was served and Johnson told Dobrynin funny stories from Texas.[45]

After the Ambassador's departure, the president immediately called an extraordinary meeting of the Council of National Security of the USA.[46] Those present were surprised at the newest events. The president told them about A. Dobrynin's visit, and about Dobrynin having informed him that the allied troops had entered Czechoslovakia on invitation of the Czechoslovak government. The event in which troops of one Communist country occupied another, friendly Communist country, was described by Johnson as aggression of one Communist country entering into the territory of another communist country. In his opinion, any kind of aggression is dangerous, and a position was therefore necessary. State Secretary Deak Rusk stated that, due to the fact the CSSR reaction was unknown, the USA did not have many possibilities, especially in the case that Czechoslovakia did nothing. He proposed that—after further conversation with Dobrynin and awareness of Czechoslovakia's reaction—the USA should adopt a written position. The president eventually approved the following steps: to invite Dobrynin and inform him that the USA would not make any statement on the Soviet offer of negotiations over the peaceful use of nuclear energy. However, they would inform him at the same time that they intended to call the UN Security Council.[47]

---

or, Anatoly Dobrynin, *In confidence. Ambassador to America's Cold War Six Presidents* (Seattle and London: University of Washington Press, 1995), 179, or Karel Durman, *Útěk od praporů: Kreml a krize impéria 1964–1991*. (Praha: Karolinum, 1998), 112.

45 FRUS 1964–1968, Volume XVII, Eastern Europe, Summary of meeting, Washington DC, August 20, 1968, 8:15–8:42 p.m.

46 Vice President Hubert H. Humphrey, UN Ambassador George Ball, CIA director Richard Helms, State Secretaries Dean Rusk and Clark Clifford, Head of United Staff Chief of Staff gen. Earle Wheeler, President's counsellor for national security Walt Rostow, Head of US Information Agency (USIA) Leonard Marks, President's Press Officer George Christian and Tom Johnson.

47 Jitka Vondrová and Jaromír Navrátil, *Mezinárodní souvislosti československé krize 1967–1970. Červenec-srpen 1968* (Brno: Doplněk, 1996), 222.

After the meeting of the Council of National Security, there were negotiations during the night between the US Secretary of State Dean Rusk and the Ambassador Anatoly F. Dobrynin. Rusk informed him that the USA were concerned about Soviet information on the invasion of Czechoslovakia, and did not understand its causes, since those mentioned by the Soviet Union—that the Czechoslovak government had asked the allies for help—were not true and he said there was no threat of an external act of aggression towards Czechoslovakia.[48]

The extraordinary meeting of the US National Security Council followed the next morning. Dean Rusk spoke about the night meeting with Dobrynin and confirmed that he had informed Dobrynin of the US position not to publish a positive statement on accepting the mentioned Soviet proposal on negotiations on atomic energy. President Johnson stated that the US Ambassador to the UN, George Ball, was given an order to express the American protest against this unjustifiable action in the UN and to insist on observance of the *UN Charter*.[49] The steps of the Administration and the President proved that, apart from verbal protests, the USA would not engage in any way. The US State Department showed an interest in gaining further information on the invasion, confirmed also by the negotiations of the Czechoslovak Ambassador to the USA, Karel Duda, who was invited to a meeting by the Deputy State Secretary and Head of the European Affairs Department, John Leddy. Leddy informed Duda of the President's night negotiations with Dobrynin, as well as about the contents of the meeting of the US National Security Council, and asked him to add some details on which the USA lacked sufficient information. In particular, the issue of the invitation of the troops, and anti-western propaganda that the CSSR faced the threat of external aggressive forces.[50] Ambassador Duda refused the Soviet interpretation about an invitation and about an external threat to Czechoslovakia, as evidenced by a message sent to the Ministry in Prague. The US government, Duda said, expressed its worries over the practice of the USSR and centred on two points in the Soviet statement: in the first place, it did not understand the part about the CSSR government request, because according to the Prague radio, the troops

---

48   Ibid., 223.
49   Ibid., 223
50   FRUS 1964–1968, Volume XVII, Eastern Europe, Telegram from the Department of State to the Embassy in Czechoslovakia, Washington DC, August 21, 1968.

entered the territory without the knowledge of the President, Prime Minister, 1st Secretary of the Central Committee KSČ and the National Assembly; and in the second place, it did not understand what those "external forces" are that are against the order of CSSR, because the US government *"does not have any information which would confirm the allegations that any non-socialist countries are involved or considering aggression against CSSR."*[51] Both sources, the American as well as the Czechoslovak one, described the negotiations of Leddy and Duda identically.

Another document, describing the Czechoslovak development, was received by the US State Department from Moscow on 21st August. The American Ambassador to the USSR, Llewellyn Thompson informed the State Department on the obtained news, stating also that many diplomats were surprised at the invasion of Czechoslovakia but others expected it even sooner. He also stated that the pro-invasion spirit prevailed in the Soviet Politburo already after the negotiations in Bratislava and there was no doubt it would happen. He described the Bratislava declaration as a tactical compromise, containing such fundamental differences that the Soviet leadership was sure Dubcek's group was inacceptable. The invasion was thoroughly timed so the maximal psychological and tactical effect of surprise was reached.[52]

On the basis of information from several sources, the American government issued on August 21, 1968 the official statement on the invasion of troops of five states of the Warsaw Pact:

> Tragic news from Czechoslovakia shocked the world. The Soviet Union and its allies invaded a country that did not defend itself, in order to suffocate the recreation of common human freedom. It is sad to see the communist way of thinking that an attempt of freedom in Czechoslovakia is considered a fundamental threat to the safety of the Soviet system. The justification of the Soviet Union is clearly unnatural. Czechoslovak government did not ask its allies to interfere in its internal affairs. Czechoslovakia was under no threat of external aggression. The action of the allies of the Warsaw Pact is a blatant breach of the UN Chart. We are consulting the other participants on what steps must be taken within the UN.[53]

---

51 Vondrová and Navrátil, *Mezinárodní souvislosti československé krize 1967–1970. Červenec–srpen 1968*, c. d., 227.

52 FRUS 1964–1968, Volume XVII, Eastern Europe, Telegram from the Embassy in the Soviet Union to the Department of State, Moscow, August 21, 1968.

53 *Public Papers of the Presidents of United States, Lyndon B. Johnson. Public Messages, Speeches and Statements of the President, 1963–1969* (Washington DC: United States Government Printing Office, 1970), 905.

The USA decried the invasion with this statement, but they merely wanted to consult the steps to be taken through the UN. And everybody knew that even if there were any UN steps, these would be on the verbal level only. The American government met due to the Czechoslovak events also during the next two days—August 22 and 23, 1968. The meeting on August 22 analysed the situation in Czechoslovakia and possible American positions arising from it as well as debated the events of the previous two days.

An employee of the President's Office, Tom Johnson summed the notes up in several points: they did not expect military intervention by the USA; the Warsaw Pact troops were ready on the borders; Dobrynin's visit to the President; the National Security Council's debates; instructions for the Ambassador George Ball; the US resolution of August 21; the USA had no obligation for military intervention; it was not either in their interest or the interest of Czechoslovakia; the Cold War had not ended. In another, more general note, Tom Johnson captured especially the speeches of the Secretaries Dean Rusk, William Wirtz and Clark Clifford. According to Tom Johnson, Dean Rusk said that one of the main reasons why the US did not expect a Soviet military intervention was the fact that the USSR would pay too high a price, especially on a political level. Supposedly, if the US decided on a military intervention, it could cause a world war. He informed the present on the negotiations of the UN Security Council and recommended the US remain active on the issue of Soviet invasion only at the level of statements.[54] In connection with similarities between Czechoslovakia and Vietnam, he did not see in the American position any relation. Also, Secretary of Labour William W. Wirtz agreed on the opinion that Czechoslovakia and Vietnam were not related but he stated that people must be confused since many did not see any difference between the invasion to Czechoslovakia and Vietnam. Secretary of Defence Clark Clifford said the US are not bound with Czechoslovakia by any treaties or agreements on mutual help, therefore, they do not have any obligation to interfere on Czechoslovak side[55]

The government meeting on the next day, August 23, was focused on a new problem—if the next target of the Soviet invasion would be

---

54 For the UN's reaction, see: Slavomír Michálek, *San Francisco 1945. Vznik Organizácie Spojených národov* (Bratislava: Veda, 2015) 158–168.
55 FRUS 1964–1968, Volume XVII, Eastern Europe, Notes of Cabinet Meeting, Washington DC, August 22, 1968.

Romania. Head of the CIA, Helms warned that the Romanian were worried of a potential Soviet military action, since Romania presented clear public support of Czechoslovakia. He suggested the US declare clearly it was not a bilateral issue between the USSR and the USA, but an issue of Moscow against the rest of the world. It was only verbal muscle-flexing, confirmed also by Rusk stating that the US did not intend any military action in support of Czechoslovakia, who had not even asked for it. Clark Clifford described the invasion of Czechoslovakia—from the military perspective—as well planned, effective and sophisticated. At the same time, he said the USSR proved it could do the same in any part of its bloc and the Soviets had a costly marine and submarine program. That was also a reason why Clifford appealed to the US responsibility to see the case of Czechoslovakia as evidence of a considerable increase in the Soviets' military power. General Wheeler reacted to Clifford, who also described the intervention in the CSSR as a fast, effective and long-term planned military operation, and gave as his evidence the detailed and exact movement of divisions in six to ten days around the the CSSR borders. He also mentioned the preparation—military training "Šumava". However, he identified some military flaws in the Soviets' approach. In his opinion, too many troops had participated in the operation—more than were necessary. Overall Wheeler came to a fundamental conclusion for the USA regarding the Soviet invasion: that the present situation proved that American could not afford to reduce her armed forces in Europe and they needed to ask their allies to improve their own.[56]

No matter how little the American administration wanted to be actively opposed to the invasion (for the reasons already mentioned), it still performed some diplomatic activities. It withdrew its ambassador for consultation and on August 25, the US Embassy in Prague issued a note requesting all American citizens to leave Czechoslovakia as soon as possible for safety reasons. The first conversations between the ambassador to Moscow, Thompson, and the State Department in Washington, were of informative nature. Ambassador Dobrynin participated in the next two conversations, on August 23 and 27. According to the memorandum of negotiations (with the participation of Dean Rusk, Llewellyn E. Thompson and

---

56 FRUS 1964–1968, Volume XVII, Eastern Europe, Summary of meeting in Cabinet Room Washington DC, August 23, 1968.

Anatoly Dobrynin), issues dealing with Czechoslovakia and broader Soviet-American relations were discussed. Dean Rusk asked Dobrynin to confirm if the American reaction to the invasion was clear to him, as it had been presented in the previous conversations. Dobrynin said the American reaction was predictable and that the decision over the military operation was not easy to reach in the USSR. At the same time, he defended the invasion as a result of internal struggles in Czechoslovakia. Rusk said there had been no evidence from Czechoslovakia that it planned to depart the Socialist camp, upon which Dobrynin replied that Alexander Dubček was weak and had lost control over the situation, a development which had led to an unsustainable sate of affairs within the Warsaw Pact. Rusk at the same time ensured the Ambassador of Kremlin on the US President's deep commitment to maintain peace. After expressing the hope that President Ludvík Svoboda's journey to Moscow would be successful, and that Alexander Dubček and the others interned in the USSR would have their safety guaranteed, Rusk changed the subject and asked Dobrynin if the information he had received was true, that there was allegedly an invasion of Romania being prepared. Dobrynin denied this. On the contrary, he said the Soviet leaders have sent cordial greetings to the Romanian representatives on the occasion of their national holiday.[57]

Another Memorandum of Conversation between A. Dobrynin and L. E. Thompson on August 27 only dealt with the newest development in Czechoslovakia. Thompson, thinking about the length of stay of the Soviet troops, asked Dobrynin how he understood the notion of "temporality". Dobrynin's answer was clear: "it will depend on how successful the Czechs are in the fulfilment of our agreement. The Soviet would naturally be glad if this period was the shortest possible".[58] Obviously, this did not correspond with the aims and intentions of the USSR to settle in Czechoslovakia. In fact, the Americans protested also on this issue—only on verbal level, without stress, and poorly. The Embassy in Prague was sending to Washington more reports on the occupation of the country but in a more or less disinterested spirit.[59]

---

57 FRUS 1964–1968, Volume XVII, Eastern Europe, Memorandum of Conversation, Dobrynin-The Secretary-Thompson, August 23, 1968.
58 FRUS 1964–1968, Volume XVII, Eastern Europe, Memorandum of Conversation, Dobrynin-Thompson, August 27, 1968.
59 A telegram from the US Ambassador to Prague, Jacob Beam, to the State Department— about the situation in Czechoslovakia. Beam describes the following particularities

An excellent American diplomat and one of the main advisers to the State Secretary Dean Rusk during this period, Charles E. Bohlen depicted the USA's dry approach to the Prague Spring and Soviet invasion, in his memoirs *Witness to History 1929–1969*. The American policy that he called the policy of disinterest, was, in his opinion, a reflection of several factors, including the fact that in Lyndon Johnson's administration there was not a uniform idea on the position of Moscow in case of an unexpected development in Czechoslovakia. Bohlen in a meeting with the State Secretary described the decision of Soviet invasion as a symbiosis of four elements. The first one was ideological—Czechoslovakia under Dubček's leadership represented the liquidation of the Soviet system. The second element was the weakening of the satellite zone around the borders with the West. The third one was Ulbricht's worries that a successful centrifugal movement in Czechoslovakia would cause similar intentions in East Germany. The fourth element or factor stated by Bohlen were Moscow's worries that this "infection" could spread from the arm—that was Czechoslovakia—Ukraine—right to the heart—the USSR.[60]

Bohlen's opinions were well founded. Although he presented them in public ex post as a private person, they contribute to our knowledge of the American Administration of that period.

George F. Kennan, former American ambassador to Moscow and author of the detention strategy, expressed a similar opinion to Bohlen's. During a private lecture tour in the Scandinavian countries, he stopped at the American Embassy in Copenhagen. There, he expressed serious worries about the irrational Soviet position in the occupied Czechoslovakia. These events obliged him and people of similar thinking to change their

---

about the situation in Prague—different forms of protest by the citizens, the limitation of public transport, the closing of petrol stations, a general strike, dialogue between the people of Prague and the Soviet soldiers about whether they knew why they are in CSSR. He stresses the increase of antipathy of the population towards the USSR and describes the occupation as bizarre. Although the troops took power in key areas, they did not declare martial law (except for some provincial towns), they did not set a military or puppet government. Although the legally created government rules, National Assembly works and the communists express their support for Dubček. In FRUS 1964–1968, Volume XVII, Eastern Europe, Telegram from the Embassy in Czechoslovakia to the Department of State memorandum of Conversation, August 24, 1968.

60 Charles E. Bohlen, *Witness to History 1929–1969* (New York: W.W. Norton and Company Inc., 1973), s. 532.

political thinking when an incorrect estimation from the past cast doubt on the Soviet reliability. According to Kennan, the whole western world will have to change its political and military construction due to the impossibility of fully revealing Soviet positions. In the light of the development, Kennan expressed the opinion that the American administration should be very cautious in its obligations towards Prague. He considered incomprehensible the compromise from Moscow between Czechoslovakia and the Soviet leaders while the occupation lasted. And Washington should publicly put pressure on Moscow for an explanation—when you have done this in Prague, what are the guarantees you will not do similar things again. Kennan also speculated on how, why and when Moscow reached the decision for the intervention. In his opinion, it was not only about a missing political guarantee from the Czechoslovak Party and government, but it also needed to get into the structures of middle groups and among the workers to gain control over the counterrevolution. In Kennan's opinion, the Kremlin was responding to the idea of individual freedom as an internal threat to the safety of the system. The loss of internal political control, too, was seen as something that could infect the whole Soviet system.[61] On this subject, he held a similar opinion Charles Bohlen.

President Lyndon Johnson presented the basic philosophy of his foreign policy in this period and also of the invasion to Czechoslovakia on 11th September 1968, when he said:

> It seems the USSR leaders have decided that the movement towards a human version of Communism in a small befriended country is a threat to their security—in spite of the fact that the Czech remained their allies in the Warsaw Pact. Since this aggressive act, the military and political threats have risen and require a closer and deeper cooperation of the western allies. We have taken undoubtedly clear steps that the use of power or power threats will not be tolerated in the spheres of joint responsibility, such as, for example Berlin.[62]

How was Czechoslovakia, occupied by the tanks of five countries, supposed to decipher this general statement from the first man of the most powerful country in the world? The US accepted the given state but regarded further power expansion from the East as a potential problem, but

---

61 National Archives and Records (NAR), f. The Czechoslovakia Crisis, 1968, The State Department's Crisis Files, Telegram from AmEmbassy Copenhagen to SecState Washington DC, No. 1922.

62 NAR, f. CIA Records, CIA-RDP79-01194A000400060001-6.

only in case it did not affect the Soviet bloc. This US position, the position of the whole democratic West, was confirmed in his messages also by Ambassador Duda from Washington. In a dispatch from 20th September 1968 for the Ministry of Foreign Affairs in Prague on the reaction of western diplomats to Czechoslovakia's event, he wrote that among the diplomats of the western countries in the USA there are strong feelings that the West should demonstrate political disagreement with the intervention of the five countries of the Warsaw Pact by selective restrictions in the bilateral relations. On the other hand, the situation of intensive Cold War should not be renewed so as not to break the results of political contacts. According to the message of Ambassador Duda, an escalation of the situation in Europe would result in a smaller space for autonomous Czechoslovak policy. In addition, the American side did not even have an interest in overstepping a certain line in the world power disputes, as it did not want to worsen Soviet-American relations. In addition, the Democrats in Congress confirmed this opinion when they publicly said that the relations between the two world powers were far more important than Czechoslovakia.[63] Karel Duda further informed the Czechoslovak Ministry of Foreign Affairs that the western diplomats prefer the idea of dialogue development between the East and the West in spite of the Soviet intervention in the CSSR.[64]

The American administration had not set a permanent position on the CSSR by the beginning of October 1968. Its only position was to accept the new reality in Czechoslovakia. The US position was confirmed by a secret dispatch of the Czechoslovak Embassy to Washington on bilateral Czechoslovak-American relations, addressed on October 10, 1968 to the Ministry of Foreign Affairs in Prague. It stated that the USA adopted a waiting position towards the USSR and the CSSR. Apart from home affairs

---

63 Thomas J. Dodd, Senator for the state, Connecticut, did not agree with the position of democratic senators in the congress. On the contrary, he requested a harsh position towards the USSR, when he asked the US in a Memorandum from September 5, 1968, to impose an immediate trade embargo on all goods from the USSR and its satellites. He further requested Johnson's administration to initiate an emergency UN General Assembly that would deal with the Czechoslovak crisis. Dodd said that the invasion was the fall of the *détente* myth. In the National Czech and Slovak Museum and Library (NCSML), Cedar Rapids, f. CNCA, box 6, Statement by senator Thomas J. Dodd on the floor of the Senate, September 5, 1968—entitled "The meaning of Czechoslovakia".

64 Jitka Vondrová and Jaroslav Navrátil, *Mezinárodní souvislosti československé krize 1967–1970, Září 1968–květen 1970* (Brno: Doplněk, 1997), 61.

(the upcoming change of administration), a decisive role was played by America's insecurity that the invasion of Warsaw Pact troops was not only an isolated, partial step, but part of a broader plan against several countries that would eventually jeapardise West Berlin. As far as Czechoslovakia was concerned, American thoughts were pessimistic as well as optimistic depending on what alternative of Czechoslovakia's future was foreseen. American opinions on the USSR were also different, depending on if it the invasion was considered a temporary episode or the return to Stalinism. According to the dispatch, the US would certainly try to use the situation in Czechoslovakia for propaganda to discredit Socialism and break the unity of the Communist movement and they already froze the contacts with the countries of "the five". In case of Czechoslovakia, they would wait further how the situation develops in the near future. For this reason, the US would "have a clear tendency not to undergo nor propose any activities from their own initiative",[65] and reason this passivity by intentions not to worsen the position of the Czechoslovak government.

In autumn 1968, the issue of Czechoslovakia appeared only sporadically in the State Department. The US Embassy telegraph from November 29, 1968 addressed to the State Department, proves this since it was only a brief evaluation of the current status of Czechoslovak-American relations. Ambassador Jacob Beam informed in it that a turn in the Czechoslovak development does not mean a complete end of the reforms and offered proposals for problem solutions that were within the bilateral issues still open and the two countries had a different view of. In the first place, he described the development of the Communist regime in Czechoslovakia from the beginning of the year, the new Party leadership, intents of an economic reform, the issues of federation, cancellation of the censorship, freedom to travel, demonstrate and the Action Programme. Regardless to the Soviet motivation, according to Beam the brutal invasion had been a shock for the Czechoslovak society on its way to a new way of life. In spite of the fact that the "socialism with a human face" still lived in the society, Alexander Dubček "has become merely a faded symbol".[66] In his opinion, Czech foreign policy was fully in accordance with the line of the

---

65 Archive Ministry of Foreign Affairs Czech Republic (AMZV ČR), Praha, Territorial Department-secret 1965–1969, USA, kart. č. 1, depeša č. 0265/68.
66 FRUS 1964–1968, Volume XVII, Eastern Europe, telegram from the Embassy to the Department of State, Prague, November 29, 1968.

Warsaw 'five', which offered Czechoslovakia a minimal space and influence in international issues.

President Richard Nixon's administration, that took office in January 1969, refused to do anything that would be an intervention in the internal affairs of the Soviet camp in the light of new political world problems of the beginning of the 70's. The rhetoric of "freeing the satellites" from the 50's was completely forgotten after August 1968 in Czechoslovakia. Nixon's administration followed the direction of Lyndon Johnson and went on building bridges with Central Europe—that is, with gradual steps to overcome the division of the old continent and replace the confrontation of the Cold War with cooperation and mutual safety.[67]

American intelligence services followed in detail the Czechoslovak reformation under the leadership of Alexander Dubček from its beginning in January 1968, and during the following months until the military invasion and its end in the summer of 1969. The intelligence service also created extensive, more general rather than analytical materials. A document with the title, *Czechoslovakia: problem of Soviet control* was created for the CIA Headquarters on January 1970 by the analyst James Ogle, and presented by the head of CIA special research committee John Kerry King. Several analysts from different CIA departments had worked on it. The material described the mechanisms and assumption of the Soviet control over Czechoslovakia, its loss in the period of time between January and August 1968, consequent military intervention and political compromise as well as the creation of preconditions for the renewal of the control from September 1968 until March 1969 and their control from April until September 1969.[68] The final evaluation of the memorandum did not contain any new facts or context. The Soviet Union, with the help of the armed forces and support of Czechoslovak conservatives established a regime that turned Prague again into an obedient and model satellite.

As a conclusion, it is necessary to evaluate the facts that influenced the US position to the invasion. Lyndon Johnson's Administration (as well as the British, French and others in the West) welcomed in the beginning the Czechoslovak reform process. At the same time, it was informed by

---

67 *US Foreign Policy in a Changing World, the Nixon Administration 1969–1973* (New York: McKay, 1973), 128.
68 NAR, College Park, MD, f. CIA Records, Intelligence Memorandum, Czechoslovakia: The Problem of Soviet Control. January 16, 1970.

Kremlin through its diplomatic representatives on the prepared invasion of the Warsaw Pact troops to Czechoslovakia. They also knew it from the information of the intelligence service, as well as from the NATO headquarters that monitored the movement of Soviet and other "befriended" troops. However, they evaluated the situation as a non-breach of American national interests or the US national security. Therefore, apart from verbal condemnation of the invasion, they did not interfere. The US simply refused to cease the fragile, gradual improvement of wider American-Soviet relations represented by the disarmament process and the peaceful use of atomic energy.

Czechoslovak crisis broke out at an inconvenient moment for the West, for the USA. The US were at that time completely engaged in Vietnam and going through a period of internal anti-war mood. In fact, Lyndon B. Johnson's administration showed clearly in the summer 1968 that it wanted to avoid the errors of Dulles's policy in the mid 50's—a policy based on preparing to "end" Soviet hegemony in Central Europe. However, Johnson's policy of "building bridges" from 1966 was never actually brought into practice. It remained only an empty phrase.

There was improvement in East-West relations in the sphere of commerce, but the US did nothing to considerably improve the situation in Central Europe. Between June and August 1968, the creators of Soviet foreign policy were sure that the US turned its "policy of bridges" into a limited American-Soviet relaxation. Another reason why Johnson's administration did not want to do anything for Czechoslovakia—not even at the time of real threat of invasion—was the Czechoslovak support (military and economic) of North Vietnam. In that time, Czechoslovakia was, after the USSR and China, the third largest supplier of Vietnam. These were also the reasons of the USA's unwillingness to support Dubček's regime. The opinions that such lack of US interest could influence the decision of the USSR to use military sources against the CSSR are not surprising. At the same time, it is not possible to claim that a different US position would have discouraged the USSR from the intervention and it really is questionable if the USA could have done such a step that would have discouraged the USSR from using its power. I believe that at that time there was no power in the world that could have ordered the Soviets of what to do in their bloc.

Just like the February coup of 1948, the invasion of 1968 too became a subject of negotiations of the UN Security Council. And just like the Prague communist coup 1948, the invasion was thanks to the Soviet veto in the UN left unattended. The resolution requesting the departure of the troops was refused. The similarity of both events lies also in the fact that the US as well as the other western powers did not act in favour of Czechoslovakia in the UN negotiations. The USA, NATO and other western structures understood the invasion of five Warsaw Pact members' troops to Czechoslovakia in the summer 1968 as an internal affair of the Soviet bloc and therefore, not an issue directed against the interest of the West.

05
Yugoslavia and Czechoslovakia During 1968

Ljubodrag Dimić
University of Belgrade, Faculty of Philosophy, Belgrade
Serbian Academy of Sciences and Arts, Belgrade

Reform attempts dominated the political landscape of Eastern Europe during the late 1960s. In an atmosphere of a rising social, political, ideological, and economic crisis, numerous dilemmas about the future development emerged. At the same time, an illusion persisted that those societies were stable, well-governed, with a secured future and social peace.

Yugoslavia had a lot of reasons to be self-absorbed during the 1960s. The crisis, which loomed over the country, was multifaceted, and in the long run, threatened the very existence of the Communist party and the joint Yugoslav state. The institutionalization of self-management led to the establishment of an economically unproductive system, which, as one of the pillars of the "Yugoslav road to socialism", became an unquestionable "dogma". Any criticism of self-management was branded by the party and state leadership as an attempt at harming Yugoslavia's reputation abroad, undermining the myth of the "Yugoslav self-management wonder", and, ultimately, bringing the independent Yugoslav model of socialism into question. The party leadership was not ready for changes.

During the 1960s the Yugoslav state was further disintegrated by an increase in the competences of individual federal republics. This process was followed by legal chaos, economic and cultural "isolationism", national homogenization, and disregard for the interests of Yugoslavia as a whole. The Yugoslav economy also became a battleground for the republican party elites. Furthermore, on the federal level, foreign debts exceeded 1.5 billion dollars. More than 30% of the total production was stockpiled. The structure of the economy was neither adapted to the needs of the domestic market, nor the export. The salaries, which were being used for "buying" social peace, were disproportionate to worker's productivity. Over 30% of the state credits were being invested in the non-profit sector. Consumption greatly exceeded the stagnating production, and the economic landscape was shaped by poor-management, carelessness, and failed investments. This all meant that economic development could not be achieved by old methods. The League of Communists of Yugoslavia (LCY) itself contributed greatly to the general crisis. As a hierarchical organization, fused with the government and state apparatus, it proved incapable of stimulating economic growth and further political democratization. In such circumstances, the changes in Czechoslovakia inevitably drew the attention of the Yugoslav leadership, desperately in need of a political compass.[69]

In 1967 the Yugoslav party and state leadership started paying closer attention to th events in Czechoslovakia. During that year Yugoslavia was visited by the Vice-President of the Czechoslovak Government, Oldřich Černík (June 1967), and President Antonín Novotný (September 1967).[70]

---

69 For more about the Yugoslav crisis during the 1960s, see: *Почетак краја СФРЈ. Стенограми и други пратећи документи проширене седнице Извршиног комитета ЦК СКЈ одржане од 14. до 16. марта 1962.* Београд 1998 [*The Beginning of an End of the SFRY. Minutes and Other Documents from the Assembly of the Executive Committee of the Central Committee of the LCY held Between 14 and 16 March 1962*, Belgrade 1998]; *VIII конгрес СКЈ*, Београд 1964 [*VIII Congress of the Central Committee of the LCY*, Belgrade, 1964]; *Четврта седница ЦК СКЈ*, Београд 1999. [*Fourth Assembly of the Central Committee of the LCY*, Belgrade 1999]; *Четрнаеста седница ЦК СК Србије*, Београд 1968 [*Fourteenth Assembly of the Contral Committee of the League of Communists of Serbia*, Belgrade 1968]; Бранко Петрановић, Момчило Зечевић, *Југословенски федерализам, II*, Београд 1987 [Branko Petranović, Momčilo Zečević, *Yugoslav Federalism*, II, Belgrade 1987]; Бранко Петрановић, *Историја Југославије, III*. Београд 1988 [Branko Petranović, *History of Yugoslavia*, III, Belgrade 1988]; Branko Petranović, *The Yugoslav Experience of Serbian National Integration*, Boulder 2002; Душан Биланџић, *Хрватска модерна повјест*. Загреб 1999 [Dušan Bilandžić, *History of Modern Croatia*, Zagreb, 1999]; Радошин Рајовић, *Уставно—правни и политички развој Србије са покрајинама*. Београд 1982 [Radošin Rajović, *Constitutional and Political Development of Serbia and its Authonomous Provinces*, Belgrade 1982]; Латинка Перовић, *Затварање круга. Исход политичког расцепа у СКЈ 1971–1972*. Сарајево 1991[Latinka Perović, *Closing the Circle. Consequences of the Political Split within the LCY 1971–1972*, Sarajevo 1991]; Љубодраг Димић, *Историја српске државности, Србија у Југославији, III*, Београд 2001. [Ljubodrag Dimić, *History of Serbian Statehood. Serbia in Yugoslavia*, III, Belgrade 2001].

70 Both sides concluded that there was "a favorable political atmosphere" between the two countries, and that "new economic conditions, which resulted from the ongoing economic reforms, enable long-term cooperation, compatible with mutual interests and levels of economic development." Museum of History of Yugoslavia (MIJ), President of the Republic's Office (KPR), I-3-a/19-13, Note on the Conversations between Josip Broz Tito and Oldřich Černík on June 2, 1967 at the Brioni island; MIJ, KPR, I-3-a/19-13,

These visits strengthened further political and economic cooperation and underlined the need for an exchange of experiences about the economic reforms.[71] Belgrade was already "well informed" about the situation in Czechoslovakia. The measures for implementing "a new economic system", changes in interior and foreign policy, attempts at finding "more elastic forms of governing", and adjusting to "the norms of the market economy" were closely observed. Belgrade was convinced that changes in the economy would inevitably lead to further democratization, which in this case meant addressing the role of the Communist party within society, liberation from party surveillance, willingness to tolerate the plurality of opinions, and the rejection of old bureaucratic (Stalinist) structures. Yugoslav Communists, faced with the same problems, were aware that reforms were needed, but were simultaneously afraid of their consequences.[72]

The old doctrine of 'the unity of action' within the Communist movement slowly started giving way to the belief that each Communist party had its own specificities. It was evident that Prague began to take "its own initiatives", and slowly approached Europe, albeit remaining politically and economically dependent on the USSR and devoted to "the common cause of the bloc".[73] Belgrade and Prague were brought together by their shared evolution of opinions towards the newly liberated countries of Africa and Asia, the shared devotion towards democratic relations among socialist states and communist parties, similar stances towards the crisis in the Middle East, and on the matters regarding the European security and defense.[74] Therefore, it seemed that 1968 might present an opportunity for Czechoslovakia and Yugoslavia to further improve their bilateral relations.

Reminder about the CSSR and the Yugoslav-Czechoslovak Relations; MIJ, KPR, I-3-a/19-13, Notes on the Conversations between President Tito and President Novotny, September 11–12, 1967; MIJ, KPR, I-3-a/19-13, Notes on the Conversations between President Tito and President Novotny on the ship "Jadranka", September 13, 1967; MIJ, KPR, I-3-a/19-13, President Novotny's speech on the ship "Jadranka", September 13, 1967.

71 Ibid.
72 MIJ, KPR, I-3-a/19-13, Reminder about the CSSR and the Yugoslav-Czechoslovak relations.
73 Ibid.
74 Ibid.

In political declarations, both sides refrained from criticism and accusations, and the economic exchange soon exceeded 200 million dollars. However, all of this did not mean that Prague did not have its reservations about Yugoslavia's socio-political system (self-management) and its foreign political orientation (non-alignment), and vice versa. Belgrade was neither fond of Czechoslovakia's bloc orientation nor of its "Stalinist" character. However, a testament to the newly achieved closeness was Tito's offer to Novotny to initiate long-term political and economic cooperation in the developing countries. This meant cooperation of companies, mutual credits, mutually funded banks, and an increase in mutual political influence in the Third World.[75] However, Novotny seemed more reserved towards this new form of "collaboration" than Josip Broz.

The Third Plenum of the Central Committee of the Communist Party of Czechoslovakia (CPC) which lasted from October 1967 to January 1968 drew close attention from the Yugoslav Party leadership, not only because important personal changes took place—namely Novotny's resignation and Alexander Dubček's ascend to power. The Third Plenum also opened "a great discussion" about the fundamental issues regarding the further development of socialism—the question whether the communist party should or could maintain the prerogatives of power in the future circumstances of the market economy.[76] Although the XII Congress of the CPC proclaimed that the Party would abstain from interfering in thw everyday work of state institutions, the long-lasting practice of party command and control of all spheres of life could not be changed overnight. Those in favor of change criticized the slow pace of decentralization. Old party cadres proved incapable of spearheading economic and social reforms, and economic sector took primacy.[77] The Yugoslav party leadership, plagued by the same problems, paid close interest to the events which unfolded in Czechoslovakia.

The CPC Plenum, which began in October 1967, was interrupted by the departure of the high-ranking party delegation to the USSR for the celebration of the 50th anniversary of the October revolution. However, neither this interregnum nor Leonid Brezhnev's sudden visit to Prague, did

---

75   MIJ, KPR, I-3-a/19-13, Notes on the Conversations between President Tito and President Novotny on the ship "Jadranka", September 13, 1967.
76   MIJ, KPR, I-5-b, CSSR Resolution of the CPC Central Committee Plenum.
77   Ibid.

drastically alter the course of the Plenum. Supported by Ulbricht and Gromyko, Brezhnev attempted to secure control over Czechoslovakia.[78] Belgrade did not look favorably on Brezhnev's visit to Prague, but approved of the fact that he "abstained from giving his opinion about the Plenum" in public. The Yugoslav party leadership was weary of certain opinions expressed at the Plenum. It did not approve of all criticism directed towards the Party, namely the accusations that it was responsible for the country's stagnation, that it had lost its revolutionary character, that it became bureaucratized, that its membership was passive, etc.[79] However, those declarations of the Plenum, which had foreseen "the unity of the whole nation", further development of socialism, "the unbreakable bond between the working class, peasantry, and the socialist intelligentsia" were favorably seen in Belgrade. The Yugoslav conviction that the reformist wing had secured victory was based on the assessment that the CPC had not abandoned its "Leninist principles", that it rejected the "accumulation of functions", and opted for "inner-party democracy".[80] The fact that "comrades" from other Socialist countries approved of the decisions adopted at the CPC Plenum seemed encouraging, despite occasional accusations of "revisionism", coming especially from East Berlin.

However, taking the whole event of the Plenum into account, Belgrade assessed that foreign political circumstances were unfavorable towards the reformist course in Czechoslovakia. The intensification of the Cold War was seen as a vital obstacle to reforms, as were the accusations from the Eastern Bloc about the rise of "revisionism", "bourgeois ideology", "anti-socialist elements", propaganda, and espionage in the CSSR. In March, 1968 a meeting of the Soviet, Bulgarian, Polish, and East German party and military delegations took place in Dresden. The Yugoslavs saw

---

[78] MIJ, KPR, I-5-b, Notes on the conversation between Mijalko Todorović and the Czechoslovak Ambassador in Belgrade on 12 January 1968; MIJ, KPR, I-5-b, Excerpts from the CPC Central Committee Plenum, 3–5 January 1968; MIJ, KPR, I-5-b, Resolution of the CPC Central Committee Plenum; MIJ, KPR, I-2, A short overview of the situation in the CSSR.

[79] MIJ, KPR, I-5-b, Notes on the conversation between Mijalko Todorović and the Czechoslovak Ambassador in Belgrade on January 12, 1968; MIJ, KPR, I-5-b, Notes on conversations between Nijaz Dizdarević and CPC Secretary V. Kautsky in Prague, January 1, 1968.

[80] MIJ, KPR, I-5-b, Excerpts from the CPC Central Committee Plenum, 3–5 January 1968; MIJ, KPR, I-5-b, Resolution of the CPC Central Committee Plenum.

it as a sign of the inevitable collapse of "bureaucratic and centralist systems", and of their desperate attempts at halting social and political changes in Czechoslovakia. Belgrade assessed that the confrontation between the "new", "progressive", and the "old", "reactionary" structures was inevitable, despite the appeasing stance of the Czechoslovak leadership. The situation was labelled as dramatic.[81]

Yugoslavs were not only concerned about internal developments in Czechoslovakia. They were convinced that the way Moscow and other Eastern European capitals would react to the events in the CSSR could challenge and even endanger some of the basic principles of Yugoslavia's foreign policy—above all, the principle of non-interference in other countries' internal affairs. The Yugoslav leadership, therefore, underlined that all problems the Czechoslovak society was facing had to be addressed by their own political elites, without foreign interference. They officially proclaimed that "socialism was inconceivable without democracy, freedom of speech, critical press, and humane relations"[82], although those same ideals were not followed in Yugoslavia.

Josip Broz Tito was further convinced that the confrontation was inevitable when the CPC adopted its *Action Programme* in April 1968. The quintessence of the *Action Programme* was expressed in the demand that the country's reforms needed to be based on "Czechoslovak conditions" while it continued also to rely on the experiences of other Socialist countries. That meant total departure from the old "mechanical and uncritical" acceptance of the methods and experiences of others—primarily the USSR. Although the *Programme* foresaw maintaining cooperation with the Soviet Union and Eastern Bloc countries, it stressed the principles of mutual respect, equality, and sovereignty. According to this document, the Czechoslovak society needed fundamental reforms, which meant an establishment of democratic social relations, reliance on uncompromised leadership, implementation of the market economy, limitation of party control, an increase in living standards, etc. Belgrade assessed that the new leadership of the CPC was not against socialism as such, but aimed at changing the manner of governing.[83] In regards to foreign policy, the "new course"

---

81 MIJ, KPR, I-2, A short overview of the situation in the CSSR; "Borba", March 1968.
82 Excerpts from an interview Marko Nikezić gave to the "Međunarodna politika" journal, "Borba", April 17, 1968.
83 MIJ, KPR, I-5-b, Report about the Action Programme of the CPC, April 30, 1968.

of Czechoslovakia foresaw wider cooperation with the world, especially with West Germany. This political orientation was different from that of the USSR and Eastern Bloc, and therefore, in the opinion of the Yugoslav diplomats, quite dangerous for the new Czechoslovak leadership.[84]

Meetings with the CSSR diplomatic and state representatives served as an opportunity for the Yugoslavs to express their political stances, and indirectly warn or even potentially influence the Czechoslovak side. They, therefore, repeatedly condemned the bloc division of the world, warned against the US imperialism, and underscored the necessity for the cooperation with newly liberated countries. Yugoslavs underlined that the policy of non-alignment served as a barrier to the "imperialist" expansion of the USA and the West, and suggested that a struggle against the bloc division of the world represented a duty for all communists. Although insisting on the fact that they were not equating Eastern Bloc with the Western one, Yugoslavs openly criticized the "reactionary" nature of the Soviet policy within the International Workers' Movement. They considered Soviet policy to be "sectarian", "outdated", and aimed at "returning to the old conceptions of monolithism and formal discipline". After the January changes took place, the Czechoslovak leadership became more susceptible to the foreign political stances of Yugoslavia, which gradually increased its prestige and potential for exercising political influence in the CSSR.[85]

In April 1968, Josip Broz Tito visited Moscow (28–30 April 1968). One of the topics of his conversations with Leonid Brezhnev, which were always open and bordering on dispute, was the "situation in Czechoslovakia". For Brezhnev, the events in Prague were "unwelcome". He was afraid that the CPC was not capable of controlling the developments in their own country, that there was fertile ground for "enemies' activities", and that the country was in turmoil. Brezhnev found the statements regarding the "outdatedness" of Marx and Lenin, the demands for "a Czechoslovak type of socialism" and especially the "blabbering" about liberalism extremely "dangerous". Unlike Tito, the Soviet leader was skeptical whether the CPC was capable of dealing with the current issues. "We fought with fascists", explained Brezhnev, "are we now supposed to give the republic to Masaryk and Beneš?" He thought that the CPC was

---

84 Ibid.
85 Ibid.

disgraced and that further concessions to the opposition needed to stop because they were nothing but a stimulus to the "counter-revolution". He spoke unfavorably about those who thought that "a new model of socialism" could be achieved within three months. Dubček was accused of opening the borders and press for spies and enemies of socialism. Brezhnev was sure that "counter-revolutionaries" aimed at overthrowing the leadership were behind the pleas of the intelligentsia within the CPC for summoning a party congress, and that a coup was being planned within the Party's own leadership. In essence, he considered the situation in Czechoslovakia not as a mere internal dispute, but as a struggle between global forces of capitalism and socialism. His words carried a clear warning: "the logic of struggle in these matters dictates that only one side can win."[86]

Some of Brezhnev's remarks on the situation in Czechoslovakia could be understood as an implicit critique of Yugoslavia's foreign political line. The Soviet leader assumed that the situation in Czechoslovakia could trigger a "chain reaction" in other socialist countries, including Yugoslavia. Therefore, Brezhnev asked Tito to "re-think together what interference in other country's affairs really meant". In Brezhnev's opinion, the duty of every socialist country was to closely observe the situation in other countries of "the socialist world". Having stated that, he openly criticized Yugoslavia's foreign and internal policy. He mentioned Yugoslav debts, unemployment, tolerance towards the enemies of socialism, and insufficient cooperation with other socialist countries. What he demanded from Tito was a "closer alliance" between the two countries, which in this case meant a common stance towards Czechoslovakia.[87]

The reactions coming from Moscow only confirmed Yugoslav initial assessment that the *Action Programme* of the CPC was a document of great significance which would inevitably lead both to the confrontation with other Communist parties and to internal divisions. Moscow's perspective regarding the events in Czechoslovakia was, in Yugoslav view, entirely negative. The Soviets were "worried" about the penetration of "anti-

---

86 MIJ, KPR, I-2, USSR, Notes on the conversations between Josip Broz Tito and Leonid Brezhnev, April 29, 1968.
87 Ibid.

socialist forces", "liberal tendencies", and growing political opposition. As a result, the leaderships of five Socialist countries convened in Moscow.[88]

Events in Prague were considered by many to be a consequence of 'Titoism'. Both in the East and the West, as well as in Czechoslovakia, there was a widespread belief that the situation was "in many ways inspired by Yugoslavia". It was also noted that the whole process did not only lead to the creation of "another model of socialism", but that Czechoslovakia was also getting closer to non-alignment. Josip Broz, albeit undoubtedly glad, aimed to define the whole affair as a consequence of internal democratization and of rejection of old antiquated forms. Tito further underlined that the development of socialism should be observed "elastically", with regards to national specificities, which dictate different roads to Socialism.[89]

Conversations with Czechoslovak political and economic representatives, which took place in May and June 1968, served as a testimony of increasing closeness between the two states. They also provided the Yugoslavs with an opportunity to get more thoroughly informed about the situation in Czechoslovakia.[90] These talks convinced the Yugoslavs that the new Czechoslovak leadership was still struggling to rid the Central Committee from "conservative forces" (Stalinists), which represented "the biggest obstacle towards further internal development". 'The conservatives' were openly supported by other Eastern Bloc countries, which gathered on July 14, 1968 in Warsaw. After this meeting, Tito became sure that an intervention in Czechoslovakia was being planned "under the pretense of the defense of socialism". His convictions were only strengthened by an increase in public allegations against the CPC throughout Eastern Europe. In Yugoslav opinion, 'extremist demands' of the Czechoslovak 'right', the 'The Two Thousand Words' manifesto, etc., only made the situation worse by providing an alibi for a military intervention. Deployment of the

---

88 MIJ, KPR, I-5-b, CSSR, Notes about the talks between the State Secretary Ljubo Babić and the Czechoslovak Ambassador to Belgrade, 9 May 1968; Notes on the conversations between Milošević and Varašek, May 16, 1968.
89 Josip Broz Tito's Interview to the Director of the European Department of the *New York Times Magazine*, Sulzberger, "Politika", May 24, 1968.
90 MIJ, KPR, I-2, CSSR, A short overview of the situation in the CSSR; MIJ, KPR, I-2, Information about the meetings among the socialist countries in April, May and June 1968, pp. 8–9.

Warsaw Pact troops on Czechoslovak territory, visits of high-ranking Soviet military officials to Prague, and announced military maneuvers of the Warsaw Pact troops on the CSSR soil only fueled Yugoslav fears. The mobilization of the Soviet public opinion against the CPC and the existence of a secret treaty which foresaw the possibility of Soviet intervention in the CSSR in the event of a threat to its security were interpreted in the same way.[91]

*

The refusal of the CPC Presidency to take part in the Warsaw meeting resembled the LCY's absence from the Cominform meeting in 1948. Yugoslav diplomacy was well informed about the contents of the telephone conversation between Brezhnev and Dubček, as well as about the wish of the Czechoslovak side for a meeting to be organized on the Czechoslovak territory, where, alongside other Eastern Bloc countries, both the LCY and the Romanian Communist Party would be present. The Yugoslav side took into account the assessment of their Ambassador to Prague Jakovlevski that the CPC leadership considered gaining "the full support of the LCY" crucial. They asked for "a meeting with comrade Tito", and aimed at providing Belgrade with first-hand information about "everything that was going on in Czechoslovakia". Furthermore, the LCY was asked to state its opinion about the ongoing situation and to notify Warsaw about its suggestion for the solution of the crisis. Tito was asked to "try to influence Ceausescu and Longo to do the same."[92]

---

[91] MIJ, KPR, I-5-b, CSSR, Report about the Action Programme of the CPC, April 30, 1968; MIJ, KPR, I-5-b, CSSR, Notes about the talks between the State Secretary, Ljubo Babić and the Czechoslovak Ambassador, May 9, 1968; MIJ, KPR, I-5-b, CSSR, Notes about the talks between the State Secretary Ljubo Babić and the Czechoslovak Ambassador to Belgrade, June 6, 1968; MIJ, KPR, I-2, CSSR, A short overview of the situation in the CSSR; MIJ, KPR, I-2, Information from the Second Department of the State Secretariat of the People's Defense about the Soviet units in the CSSR and the state of the Czechoslovak People's Army.

[92] MIJ, KPR, I-2, CSSR, Informatoon abou the meeting of the Central Committee of the CPC Presidency, 8 July 1968; MIJ, KPR, I-2, CSSR, Information about the first letter of the CPSU Central Committee, about the telephone conversation between Dubček and Brezhnev, and about certain aspects of the situation in the CSSR, 11 July 1968; MIJ, KPR, I-2, CSSR, Notes about the conversations between the Yugoslav Ambassador to

Moscow also informed Belgrade on July 11, 1968 about their assessment of the events in Czechoslovakia, and about the decisions which were to be adopted at the Warsaw meeting. It was a similar course of action the USSR undertook 12 years earlier, prior to the intervention in Hungary. The Soviets therefore attempted to make Yugoslavia at least indirectly involved in the forthcoming intervention. The "fraternal parties" of the Eastern Bloc justified their "uneasiness" and "concern" regarding Czechoslovakia with an assessment that the leadership in Prague surrendered to "the class enemies of the socialist society", that one part of the CPC Central Committee was openly advocating "a revisionist line", "giving way to anti-socialist forces", and that "a counter-revolution was taking place".[93]

However, Soviet efforts proved to be in vain. In an interview with the Egyptian journal *Al Ahram* on July 12, 1968, Tito emphasized that he "did not believe that there were short-sighted people in the USSR, who would resolve internal affairs in Czechoslovakia with force." He supported the Czechoslovak leadership by stating that the CSSR had its own army, its own party, and its own working class ready to defend socialism. On the same day, the Foreign Affairs Committee of the SFRY Federal Assembly renounced the pressure imposed on Czechoslovakia as unacceptable, and compared the current situation in Czechoslovakia with the one Yugoslavia faced in 1948. Two days later, on July 14, 1968, the LCY Central Committee notified the CPSU Central Committee that it trusted the efforts of the CPC to "further develop socialism in their country". This letter arrived in Moscow while the consultations of the socialist countries in Warsaw were underway. Belgrade considered that public support was the best way to help the Czechoslovak communists and fulfill its "internationalist duty". The letter described the reforms within the CSSR as a "significant contribution" to the general affirmation of socialism, and renounced any action "from outside" against them as a treat to the CSSR's sovereignty.[94] By supporting the CPC the Yugoslavs were in fact defending the very principles on which the independence and sovereignty of their party and state relied.

Prague Jakovlevski and Josef Smrkovský, July 12, 1968; MIJ, KPR, I-2, CSSR, Information about the situation in Czechoslovakia, July 12, 1968.

93 MIJ, KPR, I-2, CSSR, The Letter of the five Communist and workers' parties of the Socialist countries sent to the CPC Central Committee after the Meeting in Warsaw.

94 MIJ, KPR, I-2, CSSR, Reply of the CPC Central Committee on the information regarding the events Czechoslovakia, 14 July 1968.

At the meeting of the 'Warsaw Pact Five' in July 1968 in Warsaw, the intervention in Czechoslovakia aimed at defending "the counter-revolution" was openly discussed. It was clearly stated that those who had triumphed over fascism and spread socialism throughout Europe would neither allow "the historic achievements of socialism to be questioned" nor "allow imperialism to alter the balance of power in Europe in its favor".[95] It was further stated that "the defense of the rule of the working class" in Czechoslovakia demanded the following: "a resolute and courageous attack on right-wing and anti-socialist forces", "total mobilization of all means of defense", "outlawing of all anti-socialist political organizations", "the direction of mass media (...) towards the interests of the working class, workers and socialism", returning to the "principles of Marxism-Leninism". By invoking the spirit of "proletarian internationalism", and emphasizing that "there were forces capable of defending socialism" within Czechoslovakia, the letter the 'Warsaw Pact Five' sent to the CPC signaled the future intervention. The Czechoslovak leadership reacted by "rejecting the unsubstantiated claims expressed in the letter in a peaceful tone". Information about the CPC Presidency meeting, which took place on 17th July 1968, convinced the Yugoslavs that the reformist wing of the CPC was not ready to give up the impending social reforms.[96]

Meetings and conversations with leading political figures in Prague helped Belgrade get thoroughly informed about their political stances, about the internal rifts within the CPC Central Committee, as well as about the conversations between Prague and Moscow. In such a precarious situation, pressures of any kind would, in Yugoslav opinion, only further complicate the internal issues of Czechoslovakia. The Soviet support for "healthy forces" within the CPC was understood in Belgrade as a "call to rebellion". Therefore, the letter from Warsaw was not only seen as an attack on Czechoslovakia, but as a possible threat to Yugoslavia as well.

The meeting of the LCY Central Committee on July 16, 1968 was dedicated to the events in Czechoslovakia. Yugoslavia officially

---

95 MIJ, KPR, I-2, CSSR, The Letter of the five Communist and workers' parties of the Socialist countries sent to the CPC Central Committee after the Meeting in Warsaw.
96 MIJ, KPR, I-2, CSSR, The Letter of the five Communist and workers' parties of the Socialist countries sent to the CPC Central Committee after the Meeting in Warsaw; MIJ, KPR, I-2, CSSR, The letter of the Central Committee of the CPC, sent to Leonid Brezhnev on 15 July at 16h, before the end of the ongoing meeting.

proclaimed that the impending events were "a clear testament that the principles of the Belgrade declaration of 1955 and the Moscow declaration of 1956 were still relevant and righteous."[97] A few days later the Yugoslav side thoroughly analyzed the reply of the CPC Central Committee to the letter from Warsaw. Yugoslavia supported the Czechoslovak position, and the reply was published in the official party newspaper *Borba* on 19th July.[98] Although the Yugoslavs looked favorably on the fact that the Soviets agreed to hold the next bilateral meeting in the CSSR, rather than in the USSR, they were convinced that both sides would remain on "current positions".[99]

Yugoslav (and Romanian) support was of utmost importance to the Czechoslovak party and state leadership during the summer of 1968. The CSSR, therefore initiated several agreements with the Yugoslav side foreseeing mutual cooperation, friendship and formation of Yugoslav-Czechoslovak societies.[100] The visit of Josip Broz Tito to Prague on August 9–10 1968 served several purposes. On the one hand, it was a public demonstration of Yugoslavia's support for Czechoslovakia, and on the other hand, it was intended to promote Yugoslav independent foreign political orientation. During the visit, Dubček informed the "Yugoslav comrades" about the internal changes within the CPC, the activities of "anti-socialist forces", the steps taken to pacify the current situation and further plans for the development and democratization. In the agreement, Tito accepted that no "counter-revolution" was taking place in Czechoslovakia. However, he warned Dubček that "allowing democracy to those who are against socialism" would in fact mean "allowing chaos". He openly spoke about his "errors" in dealing with "internal enemies of socialism" in Yugoslavia, and

---

97 MIJ, KPR, I-2, CSSR, Information about the publicity given to the letter of the LCY in the Czechoslovak mass media.
98 MIJ, KPR, I-2, CSSR, The Central Committee of the CPC meeting, July 17, 1968; MIJ, KPR, I-2, CSSR, Meeting of the CSSR Government, July 18, 1968, "Borba", July 19 1968.
99 MIJ, KPR, I-2, CSSR, The overview of the situation prior to the meeting between the CPC and the CPSU.
100 MIJ, KPR, I-2, CSSR, Note about the initiative of the CSSR for signing a friendship treaty between SFRY and CSSR; MIJ, KPR, I-2, CSSR, Note about the initiative of the CSSR about the creation of the Yugoslav-Czechoslovak society; MIJ, KPR, I-2, CSSR, Note about the Prague TV broadcast on July 17, 1968 about the anniversary of the Cominform Resolution.

encouraged Dubček to take "radical steps" towards the opposition.[101] Tito thought that the situation in Czechoslovakia was not overly dramatic and expressed his trust in the capabilities of the CPC and the working class to "combat the internal enemies of socialism". Any interference in Czechoslovak affairs would, in his opinion, be a grave error, which would only further compromise Socialism.[102] Tito returned to Belgrade with an impression that the Czechoslovak leadership had reached the "right conclusions" and that it was fully resolved to combat the enemies of socialism.[103]

The fact that Tito's visit to Prague was not extensively covered in the Eastern Bloc press was a clear sign to Belgrade that there was no hesitation in regards to Czechoslovakia. During those days "Pravda" was full of articles about the "obligations" of Marxist-Leninist parties to provide "fraternal countries" with aid and protection in case of "imperialist" involvement in their internal affairs. The editorials of that journal, which always represented the Kremlin's positions, preached an "unsolvable conflict" between Marxism-Leninism on one side, and "bourgeois-liberal" and "pseudo-revolutionary" attitudes on the other. A swath of sensational articles about the "secret Western plans" for a "lightning fast occupation of East Germany" was circulating in the Eastern press. In this light, numerous reports from Czechoslovakia testified to the rising propagandist and political pressure, as well as to a possible military intervention.

During the night between August 20 and 21, history, alongside Soviet tanks, turned in the wrong direction. Josip Broz Tito reacted to these events by assembling a special session of the Presidency and the Executive Committee of the LCY Central Committee in the evening of August 21 on the Brioni Island. Two days later the LCY Central Committee assembled in Belgrade. Tito and other leading Yugoslav communists rejected the claims that the military intervention was caused by the need to defend the western borders of Czechoslovakia. The reasons behind the "occupation" of Czechoslovakia were in their opinion both political and ideological in nature. The Eastern Bloc parties' decision to intervene was interpreted as a result of their bureaucracies' inherent fear of inner-party democrati-

---

101 Primarily, towards the K213, the KAN group, and Social-Democratic Party.
102 MIJ, KPR, I-2, CSSR, Talks between Dubček and Tito, August 9–10 1968.
103 Archives of Yugoslavia (AJ), Central Committee of the LCY (CK SKJ), III/134—Attachment No. 2, Minutes from the XI joint session of the LCY Presidency and the Central Committee of the LCY Executive Committee on 21 August 1968 on the Brioni Island.

zation. The Yugoslavs firmly believed that their main aim was to prevent Czechoslovakia from "following its own internal course". While commenting on the intervention in Czechoslovakia, Tito stated: "this is not only about Czechoslovakia, we are in question, as well". He was convinced that the Eastern Bloc countries considered Yugoslavia to be the main inspirator, initiator and protagonist of what was going on in Prague, and that, therefore, the main target of the attack was Yugoslavia itself. He further stated that the intervention was a warning to other socialist countries as well.[104] Fearing the intentions of both East and West, Tito called for unity and solidarity among the LCY membership, and announced taking measures which would put all enemies "under control"—"we will not refrain from arresting them if we have to", stated Tito.[105]

Tito's protest against the military intervention in Czechoslovakia was at the same time a call to defend Yugoslavia. By declaratively protecting the general principles of international relations and reaffirming the interests of world socialism, Tito was in the first place trying to defend the internal and foreign political position of his own country. He considered the intervention in Czechoslovakia to be a threat to "the very independence of our country", and therefore appealed to his compatriots to "remain calm", "to prevent panic and unrest", but to make clear to all potential aggressors that the Yugoslavs would defend their own country until the end. Tito promised that any traitor within the army ranks would be immediately arrested. Civilians supporting the enemy would be punished as well—"feathers would fly", he warned. Tito further assessed that the intervention in Czechoslovakia was a sign that a "neo-Stalinist line" triumphed in the USSR, and was therefore resolute that "we have to be our own masters". He considered the official cause of the intervention (the appeal to the USSR by a group of workers in an automobile factory) especially dangerous, as he was afraid of a similar scenario in Yugoslavia. He feared that "rankovićevci" could,[106] instigated by the Soviet Union, make a similar appeal, and therefore sarcastically stated that "those healthy forces" had to be neutralized. On the other hand, those who harbored "pro-Western

---

104 Ibid.
105 Ibid.
106 Followers of Aleksandar Ranković, the long-term Minister of Interior, chief of the intelligence agency and Vice-President of Yugoslavia, who fell from power and was expelled from the LCY in 1966.

illusions" had to be "crushed" as well, since he thought the West feasted on the current situation like a "vulture".[107]

The severity of these events forced Tito and the LCY leadership to once more reconsider the Czechoslovak crisis on August 23, 1968.[108] They reached several conclusions. The official Soviet interpretation of the military intervention was again rejected. The real reason behind the intervention was found in the fear from the "efforts towards democratization" made by the new Czechoslovak leadership. However, Tito was sure that the main goal of the Soviets was not Czechoslovakia but Yugoslavia. He reminded the members of the Central Committee about his last visit to Moscow, and the Soviet warnings he received about the situation in Yugoslavia. Although he accepted that certain problems in fact existed in Yugoslavia, he rejected any foreign interference in Yugoslav affairs.[109] All of this testified that the state and national security of Yugoslavia were in jeopardy. The membership of the LCY was asked to defend the independence and free development of Yugoslavia against all threats, "regardless from which side they might come". The benevolent attitude of the USSR towards Yugoslavia was a thing of past, Tito concluded.[110]

Soon, the perceived threat to Yugoslav independence overshadowed the events in Czechoslovakia. The general attitude that there would be no abandoning of the "independent road to socialism" was once again reaffirmed, and as a result the relations with the USSR and the Eastern Bloc remained "frozen" for a while. At the same time, social and economic reforms in Yugoslavia were also halted. Military readiness was raised to the highest level. Party propaganda successfully harnessed the patriotic feelings amongst the Yugoslav communists to bolster its ranks. This resulted in an influx of more than 175,000 new party members, 125,000 of which were from the youth.

Although in late 1968 internal Yugoslav reports concluded that the threat from the USSR was "real", during the Spring of 1969 the assessments began to change. This change was a consequence of the mutual awareness

---

107 AJ, CK SKJ, III/134—Attachment 2, Josip Broz Tito's speech, 33–36.
108 AJ, CK SKJ, II/35, Minutes from the 10th Session of the Central Committee of the LCY, August 23, 1968.
109 AJ, CK SKJ, III/134—Attachment 2, Josip Broz Tito's speech; AJ, CK SKJ, II/35, Minutes from the 10th Session of the Central Committee of the LCY, August 23, 1968.
110 Ibid.

of Moscow and Belgrade that the current situation had to be resolved. After its intervention in Czechoslovakia, the USSR aimed to pacify the situation in Europe and to re-open the dialogue about European security and defense. For Moscow, it was not only about "rehabilitating" its policy in Europe. The reasons were multifaceted: the Sino-Soviet confrontation, complex Soviet-American relations, disobedience within the Eastern Bloc, the waning of the appeal of global communism, high military expenditure, and economic and social difficulties within the USSR.[111]

The Yugoslav leadership was well aware that the Soviet Union still "wanted to influence and to achieve long-term ideological, political, economic and military presence" in Yugoslavia. The willingness of the USSR to reapproach Yugoslavia was therefore understood as an integral part of global Soviet foreign policy. However, Tito considered "a constructive dialogue" which would improve the relations between the two countries crucial. In his opinion, the historical processes, which lead to further political stabilization in Europe, were in favor of Yugoslavia. He saw the establishment of good political relations with the Soviet Union as an important part of these processes. An improvement of these relations would not only strengthen the Yugoslav position towards East and West, but also within the international workers' movement. The wholehearted support for the Prague reformists, therefore, became a thing of past.

---

111 MIJ, KPR, I-3-a, SSSR, Information about the first day of the conversations between the State Secretary for foreign affairs of the SFRY Mirko Tepavac and the Soviet Foreign Minister A. Gromyko, September 3, 1969; MIJ, KPR, I-2-a, SSSR, Notes about the conversations between Josip Broz Tito and A. Gromyko at the Brioni island, September 4, 1969; Ljubodrag Dimić, Yugoslavia and Security in Europe during the 1960s (Views, Attitudes, Initiatives), *Токови историје*, 2016/3, 9–42.

06
Towards Military Intervention. Prague Spring and Party Representatives in Hungary

Miklós Mitrovits
Institute of History, Research Centre for the Humanities, Budapest

Historians have been interested for a long time in how the Hungarian Socialist Workers' Party (MSZMP) under the leadership of János Kádár passed from initial support for Alexander Dubček and the Prague Spring to approval by the Hungarian popular army, together with the armies of the Warsaw Pact, then participation in the military intervention against Czechoslovakia. This meant the end of the Czechoslovak process of reformation. In the following study, we shall present the most important milestones of those events.

Hungarian and Czechoslovak reforms of the 60's had many common features. When Alexander Dubček became head of the Communist Party of Czechoslovakia (KSČ) it was obvious that the Hungarian reforms differed considerably from the Czechoslovak ones. Czechoslovak reform processes, known as the 'Prague Spring', were created as a result of de-Stalinization, which ended in 1956. Dubček had the support of the whole Czechoslovak society, which put pressure on the party leadership. Dubček could not politicize by excluding the public, and isolate the reforms from social influence. However, Hungary managed to enforce Stalinization to a certain level. The vast majority of Hungarian society got used to the situation after 1956 and not only agreed with it but there underwent a certain '*reconciliation*' with Kádár's leadership. The reforms ran in conjunction with no social pressure in their direction and their pace depended exclusively on the political leadership.

Tandem Dubček—Kádár

Dubček was appointed 1st Secretary of the Central Committee of the Communist Party (ÚV KSČ) on January 5. 1968. The first official visit of newly appointed members of the party leadership was usually to Moscow. Before

Dubček went to Moscow, he informed Kádár he wanted to meet him. The meeting took place on the 20th–21st of January 1968 in Palárikovo and in Komárno. The fact that Dubček prioritized Kádár to Brezhnev was an expression of Czechoslovak leadership's distrust of Moscow and at the same time a sign of trust towards Budapest. At the same time also, for the Hungarian party leader it was an excellent opportunity to adopt his own attitude towards the events in Czechoslovakia, and he hoped he would have influence on Dubček.

Kádár was interested in the ideas of the new 1st Secretary ÚV KSČ because he was worried about the messages arriving from the neighbouring countries. Kádár summarized his impressions saying: "It is correct that we accepted the proposal of comrade Dubček, it was an open and honest conversation. Comrade Dubček is a communist with sane, sober and responsible thinking who faces problems"[112]

After Dubček's trip to Moscow,[113] they met again with Kádár on the February 4. 1968. The Czechoslovak politician informed him that the *Action Programme of the Communist Party of Czechoslovakia* (Akčný plán KSČ) would be ready at the end of March. Kádár replied with a warning: "to be careful since everyone creates an action programme". Two days later, during the meeting of the political committee MSZMP, he also said that several social groups have programmes that go far beyond the boundaries of current opinions within ÚV KSČ. Kádár and Dubček agreed that "the conditions for future development of Czechoslovak-Hungarian relations and cooperation are favourable."[114] Kádár invited Dubček to Budapest. 1st Secretary ÚV KSČ proposed the renovation of the Czechoslovak-Hungarian Treaty on Friendship, Cooperation and Mutual help during the year 1968, which was valid until 1969. In his opinion, a new treaty would

---

112 MNL OL [National Archives of Hungary], M-KS 288. f. 47/743. ő. e. Similar description was presented during the meeting of the political committee ÚV KSSZ on the 18th January 1968 by the Soviet Ambassador to Prague, Stepan Chervonenko. "Comerade Dubček is without doubt an honest, loyal man, a devoted friend of the Soviet Union" Quotation: Pihoja, 1998. 8.

113 The meeting took place during January 29–30, 1968. Secretary General of PB CPSU, Leonid Brezhnev ensured the Czechoslovak leadership on his full support. Document about debates, see: Vondrová—Navrátil, 1995. 39–43.

114 NA ČR [National Archives of the Czech Republic], KSČ-ÚV-02/1. sv. 60. a.j. 67/kinf10.; MNL OL, M-KS 288. f. 5/445. ő. e.

express the narrow cooperation between Czechoslovakia and Hungary.[115] At that time, Kádár did not agree yet with the treaty renewal but he later changed his mind. He expressed his support for the Czechoslovak leadership and in his opinion, also the other socialist countries would agree on the position of Hungarian and Soviet leadership on the events in Czechoslovakia.[116]

Kádár thought of Dubček without prejudice and considered him a talented politician. Dubček was far more open-minded than Novotný, he knew about the Slovak situation and he even spoke Hungarian a little. Kádár also hoped that Dubček could correct the insufficiencies of the previous economic reform and control the group that requested political changes. If he managed to enforce his intentions, it would create favourable international conditions for the approval of Hungarian reforms from January 1, 1968.

"… take into consideration our experience with the counterrevolution of 1956!"

The first serious problems appeared on the 5th April 1968, after the approval of *Action Programme ÚV KSČ* that Dubček had mentioned already during the February meeting. The document was sent to the leading representatives of Socialist countries, Kádár too. The leaders of the member states of the Warsaw Pact agreed on a mutual position according to which the *Action Programme* contained such radical changes they could not agree with. This was the reason why the head representatives of the parties met in Dresden on 23rd March. Another motivation for the summit was the news of the alleged plan to dismiss Novotný, who was set to remain president until the end of January.[117]

The political committee MSZMP had dealt with this situation already on its meeting on March 19. Kádár stated "the Czech do not insist too much for negotiations in Dresden. As far as me concerned, if comrade Dubček sends a notice, we will meet". The leadership in Budapest was of

---

115 MNL OL, M-KS 288. f. 5/445. ő. e.
116 NA ČR, KSČ-ÚV-02/1. sv. 60. a.j. 67/kinf10.
117 On the background of the summit, see: Békés, 2008; Huszár, 1998. 26–33. Brezhnev convinced Kádár during several weeks on the necessity of this meeting. The Hungarian party leader on the contrary tried to reduce the caused tension. Dresden was in the end suggested by Dubček as a "neutral place".

the opinion that the Hungarian delegation could not influence Ulbricht and Gomulka and Czechoslovakia did not support this meeting. He also said that the ÚV KSČ plenary was to meet in three of four days and the approval of the Action Programme was a ready-made thing, so the Czechoslovak leadership could not be convinced to change its attitude. After the debate, Kádár came to the conclusion that "we will not interfere in the internal affairs of Czechoslovakia nor will we propose any position to them (…) let us tell comrade Brezhnev that we are in favour of meeting, but we are not so eager and we are rather sceptical (…) one cannot interfere in the Czech events, but we can influence their further development."[118] Kádár called Brezhnev on the same day in the evening, saying the MSZMP leadership did not see any reason for meeting in Dresden. However, they would participate.[119]

In the meantime, (20th March) Antonín Novotný resigned from the position of president. On the next day, the political committee of the CPSU met and decided on the adoption of particular measures for stopping Czechoslovak reform processes.[120] The Secretary General of the Soviet party said that "in order to solve this issue, it is necessary to think in detail the particular steps, we also mean the use of the same solution as in the Hungary case." Alexander Shelepin mentioned that during the meeting in Dresden, "it would surely be convenient if Kádár reminded the Czech of the Hungarian events."[121] The Head of the Council of Ministers, Alexei Kosygin, was also talking about the events of 1956 when he said "it was necessary to find new power that we could rely on".

After these events, on the 23rd March the leading representatives of six parties met in Dresden. The KSČ leadership was united in its position in the subject of Czechoslovak processes of reformation—not only Dubček, Jozef Lenárt and Drahomír Kolder but also Vasil Biľak who was known as a great supporter of the USSR. Gomulka had a flaming speech on the "counterrevolution freely wandering in Czechoslovakia", while Brezhnev presented the same criticism of the reform wing of KSČ as the one heard in the meeting of the political committee of the CPSU.

---

118   MNL OL, M-KS 288. f. 5/451. ő. e.
119   MNL OL, M-KS 288. f. 47/743. ő. e.
120   Pihoja, 2000. 276.
121   Quotations from the minutes in Hungarian, see: Huszár, 1998. 42–50

Kádár was more subtle; he acted more in defence of Czechoslovakia against the military East German and Polish political representatives. First he thanked Dubček for his speech, and then he said that as far as the internal situation in the Czechoslovak party was concerned, "the right to present decisions belongs to the Czechoslovak comrades and we do not want to and cannot interfere."[122] At the same, he said "important events happening in one of the socialist countries are connected with the internal events in the other socialist countries". He came to the conclusion that "we must help each other and cooperate" and therefore he considered important Hungary showed solidarity towards the present Czechoslovak leadership. If five parties were to support the KSČ, they need to have exact information on what was happening in Czechoslovakia. Kádár wanted to explain why the meeting in Dresden, but at the same time there were intentions to distract from the fact that the Czechoslovak leadership participated in some kind of 'trial'.

In accordance with the said during the meeting of the political committee of the CPSU, Kádár also mentioned Hungary's experience in 1956. He stressed that the Hungarian party had not used in any context the term "counterrevolution" in relation to the development in Czechoslovakia. According to the Hungarian leadership, the situation in this country very much reminded of the Hungarian development from February until October 1956 "when there was not counterrevolution (…) in Hungary, until the 23rd October there were no counterrevolutionary elements". In relation with Imre Nagy he said "that person was neither an agent nor a counterrevolutionary in the meaning of wanting to end socialism in Hungary (…) he became an enemy on 25th or 26th October 1956 when he became part of the enemy side and there was no way back from there."[123]

János Kádár's perception is interesting also from the point of view that in the resolution of ÚV MSZMP from 5th December 1956, as a cause

---

[122] Kádár's speech in Dresden quotated by Vondrová—Navrátil, 1995. 96–99., records of the Polish party quoted by Garlicki—Paczkowski, 1995. 53–54. The Hungarians did not make any minutes, during the meeting of the political committee MSZMP on April 2 Kádár only mentioned his speech in three sentences. But we do have Kádár's handwritten notes on one page: MNL OL, M-KS 288. f. 47/743. ő. e. Tibor Huszár did not know the earlier Czech and polish sources when writing his book (1997–1998) and therefore he did not use them. Viď: Huszár, 1998. 50–59.

[123] See: Vondrová—Navrátil, 1995. 97–98.

of the counterrevolution, it was stated that "Imre Nagy and his fellows began to organize a secret anti-state conspiracy in December of 1956, the aim of which was to take over the power and overthrow the Hungarian Popular Republic."[124] Kádár contradicted his own political theory in order to defend the Czechoslovak reform process and free it from any suspicion of counterrevolutionary. At the same time he said that "similar events can change any of us into Imre Nagy."[125] That was a sign for Dubček and the Czechoslovak leadership to understand the limits. "Comrades, take into account our experience with the counterrevolution of 1956 because we paid for it with our blood."[126]

In Dresden, there was no open dispute because Brezhnev and the Soviet leadership, opposed to their previous statements, ensured the "Czechoslovak brethren party" on their full trust. There was no direct intervention in Czechoslovak internal affairs yet. Kádár and the Hungarian delegation made sure also that the Soviet proposal was refused and the communiqué contained a compromise.[127]

But the Soviet leadership did not want to give up on its policy of coercion. On the 4th of May, a four-member delegation travelled to Moscow, Dubček, Černík, Smrkovský and Biľak. Marshall Ivan Jakubovski informed them that the Soviet Union planned to perform a Command-Staff exercise in the territory of Czechoslovakia. The delegation agreed with this plan. During the meeting, the Soviets also clearly expressed that "in case of worsening of the situation, the Soviet Union will give up on its neutral position and in the interest to maintain a socialist Czechoslovakia will undergo the most far-reaching steps."[128]

Two days later also the heads of the parties and the Prime Ministers of the other Socialist countries travelled to Moscow so Brezhnev could inform them of the results of the debates with the KSČ delegation. Kádár kept the same position as during his speech in Dresden.[129] He repeated that

---

124 See: *A Magyar Szocialista Munkáspárt határozatai és dokumentumai*, [Documents and resolutions of the Hungarian Socialist Popular Party]), 1964. 13–17.
125 This sentence appears in the minutes of the Polish party, see: Garlicki—Paczkowski, 1995. 53.
126 Vondrová—Navrátil, 1995. 98–99.
127 Huszár, 1998. 58–59.
128 Quoted by: Huszár, 1998. 80–81.
129 See Kádár's speech in: Vondrová—Navrátil, 1995. 201–205.

the MSZMP did not consider the Czechoslovak reform processes as counterrevolutionary. He insisted the problems should not be solved with arms. He reminded attendees also that in 1956 the presence of the Soviet armies had been used as "a good excuse" for the outbreak of counterrevolution.[130] Kádár defended Dubček again, who, in his opinion, fought with the past—that is to say that the current situation was created due to the mistakes of the leadership of Novotný's era. He stressed that certainly in Czechoslovakia there were those who needed help. Dubček, Kolder and the others were in an extraordinary situation. They had to fight on two fronts, on one hand against the mistakes of the past, on the other hand "against the enemies of socialism, the counterrevolution and imperialist agents". Kosygin interrupted Kádár asking him what he thought of the Action Programme KSČ. The Hungarian leading representative of the party did not get out of the concept. He said he considered the programme "a big nothing". Everyone can take of it what they like.[131] "This programme represents a general socialist compromise."

Kádár also supported the military training planned by Brezhnev. "The longer it takes, the better (...) The military training must take place and we will participate. However, I do want to state that our principal task is to enforce the core of the KSČ leadership and in case this leadership is incapable, new people need to be found to replace it."[132]

Kádár's position was modified after Dresden in two fundamental ways. On one side he announced that Hungarian troops would participate in the military training in the territory of Czechoslovakia, which definitely had a political undertone and which would to a large extension influence the balance of power in the KSČ leadership. On the other hand, he declared for the first time that he could imagine changes in the Czechoslovak leadership.

---

130 MNL OL, M-KS 288. f. 5/455. ő. e. We need to say Kádár said this for the first time. On 15th December 1956, eleven days after the defeat of the Hungarian revolution, Kádár said something similar during his debate with the Czechoslovak Prime Minister Viliam Široký. Bencsik—Mitrovits, 2018. 421–431.

131 Kádár presented his slightly modified opinion on the Action Programme to Dubček also during the June visit of the Czechoslovak party and governmental delegation in Budapest (see further).

132 Vondrová—Navrátil, 1995. 204–205.

Dubček in Budapest

Between May 29 and June 1, 1968, another Central Committee KSČ plenary took place that decided on the extraordinary congress of KSČ where new members of the Central Committee were to be elected. During the meetings of district and municipal committees, it became clear that those who supported Moscow could lose their membership. This fact was also perceived by the Hungarian leadership of the party and it affected also the preparations for the visit of the Czechoslovak delegation for the renewal of the Czechoslovak-Hungarian treaty on friendship, cooperation and mutual help. This was not an obvious fact since a short time before the military training of member states of the Warsaw Pact in the territory of Czechoslovakia was approved. Apart from that, the treaty signed in 1949 was to be prolonged until 1969 so its early signing was not only of legal but also of symbolic importance.

The delegation led by Dubček and Černík arrived in Budapest on the 13th June 1968 and already during the first day they had held long debates with the Hungarian leading representatives.[133] The situation turned complicated due to the fact that on the same day, Osvald Machatka's article "Another anniversary"/"Také jedno výročí"/ was published in the magazine Literární listy. The text was written on the 10th anniversary of the execution of Imre Nagy and its content contradicted to what Kádár's ideology and propaganda stated. The author of the article was cautious not to mention Kádár's name but everybody knew that the first man in MSZMP played a decisive role in Nagy's execution. Kádár mentioned the article to the Czechoslovak delegation, not during the official debates but later, during dinner.[134] It was obvious he wanted to avoid a scandal because of the article.

During the official debates Kádár did not express only criticism and his worries but he also clearly stated that MSZMP expressed "confidence and solidarity" for KSČ. "The manner, time and way" the Czechoslovak leadership would solve the accumulated problems was their thing. "We agree with everything that strengthens socialism. What we do not agree

---

133 MNL OL, XIX-J-1-j Csehszlovákia (Czechoslovakia), 1968. év (year). 23. doboz (box). 001169/35. a 001169/36.
134 MNL OL, XIX-J-1-j Csehszlovákia (Czechoslovakia), 1968. év (year). 23. doboz (box). 001169/34.ß

with? What we think that weakens the positions of socialism", said Kádár.¹³⁵

Dubček thanked the Hungarian leadership for their understanding of the situation, then informed in extension on the past period and as a conclusion stated:

> Different rightist, antisocial elements cannot influence and do not influence the events. Precisely because of that, we stated clearly during the January and February meetings of ÚV KSČ that the most fundamental task is to strengthen the leading power of the party. In addition, it is clear that we shall further support the relations with the Soviet Union and we shall not allow them to worsen, the same goes about the socialist countries. (...) It is not any kind of democracy, our aim is to build a socialist democracy.¹³⁶

Kádár reacted to certain points. In his opinion, the resolutions approved on during the January and February ÚV KSČ meetings, including personnel changes and the Action Programme, belong to internal issues of KSČ: "We cannot do anything else but take note on them". Kadár had nothing against the May plenary, nor the planned extraordinary congress. However, he reminded Dubček that not everyone who says so is truly also a defendant of Socialism.

Dubček agreed with this, he thought that the times would come when violence will be necessary to intervene against the enemies. Kádár did not exclude such a possibility and at the same time agreed with his partner that it is necessary to imprison and punish those who "violate socialist law". At the end, he expressed "a wishful thought": "we have reached the point where we had to make politics with cannons, I do hope you will avoid that."

During the two-day visit, there were several one-to-one talks. Dubček mentioned the debate in Moscow on the 6th May, to which the Czechoslovak delegation had received no invitation and he did not like the plan of a military training. Kádár tried to calm him by saying he had told the Soviets about "the dangers hidden in the presence of the Soviet army in Czechoslovakia which could cause unnecessary nationalist reactions."¹³⁷

---

135 NA ČR, KSČ-ÚV-02/1. sv. 75. a.j. 101/9.; MNL OL, XIX-J-1-j Csehszlovákia (Czechoslovakia), 1968. év (year). 23. doboz (box). 001169/36.
136 Ibid.
137 MNL OL, XIX-J-1-j Csehszlovákia (Czechoslovakia), 1968. év (year). 23. doboz (box). 001169/44.

While the meeting Kádár in an uneasy position, the Czechoslovak delegation came out of it feeling content. The minutes for the meeting of the ÚV KSČ leadership, that was to take place on 3rd July state that "the debate and dialogue ran in an honest, friendly atmosphere, they showed comrade explicitness and mutual understanding, we agreed on all issues".[138] The participants stated that the Hungarian party had expressed its solidarity with KSČ and the reform process in Czechoslovakia. The Hungarian party was also ready to offer help in such a form that Czechoslovakia considered adequate and necessary.

Military training Šumava

During the Czechoslovak-Hungarian meeting, an event was mentioned that only particular people knew about: a strategic-military training of commanders in the territory of Czechoslovakia, with the cover name Šumava. Dubček agreed with it willy-nilly on the 4th May during his conversation with Brezhnev, two days later the plan of a military training was approved also by the leading representatives of five socialist countries during the debate in Moscow.

From the member states of the Warsaw Pact, the Soviet Union, Czechoslovakia, Poland, German Democratic Republic and Hungary participated in this military training.[139] When it ended, the Hungarian Minister of Defence openly stated that the aim, content and course of the training were marked by different positions of the participating countries on the development of the political situation in Czechoslovakia. "The atmosphere was often tense and contradictory, which was obvious especially in the verbal attacks of the Czechoslovak hosts with Soviet comrades who led the training." It was not surprising since the military training Šumava had the aim to interfere with the internal situation and a masked preparation of the occupation. This fact was also stated by the Minister of Defence Lajos Czinege: "The intention of the great military training was that the armies of several countries got further experience in the field of planning, organization, leading and cooperation (…) During the training, the Soviet commanders based on the assumption that there was counterrevolution in Czechoslovakia or it is at the beginning of counterrevolution. The party

---

138   NA ČR, KSČ-ÚV-02/1. sv. 75. a.j. 101/9.
139   HL [Military History Archives in Budapest], MN 1968—Zala, 4. doboz (box), 8. ő. e.

and the government are not united, they tolerate counterrevolutionary and anti-Soviet propaganda and conspiracy. State security does not intervene in the internal reaction (…) Czechoslovak military commanders could not fully participate in the military training and protested." The Soviets did not offer the Czechoslovak military commanders any information "on aims, beginning, end, task description, performance plan, times of particular trainings nor on the number of military units and command staff."[140]

23,721 soldiers, 6344 vehicles, 279 tanks, 87 planes and helicopters participated in the military training in the territory of Czechoslovakia. If we add the troops that trained in the territories of Germany, Poland, Hungary and the Soviet Union, there were 30,000 to 40,000 participants.[141] The Hungarian People's Army was represented by the 5th armada and 11th moto rifle division, together 800 persons and 260 military vehicles.[142] The Hungarians represented only a 3.37% of soldiers present during the military training in Czechoslovakia. During this training, the Minister of Defence Lajos Czinege met his Czechoslovak colleague Martin Dzúr and the president Ludvík Svoboda. Marshall Ivan Jakubovski kept looking for excuses so he did not have to meet them. The military training eventually ended on July 2 and the Hungarian troops left the country on the next day.[143]

Kádár was in Moscow at that time, because between the 27th June and the 4th July he headed the Hungarian delegation during the official visit to the Soviet Union where, naturally, the situation in Czechoslovakia was debated. The Soviets presented a large number of complaints on the Czechoslovaks: "they keep going to the right", "the attacks against the regime sharpen", "counterrevolutionary powers stronger" and claimed the

---

140 The report with the above mentioned statements was created by Deputy Minister of Defence, Gen. István Oláh and Substitute Chief of Staff, Gen. Ferenc Szűcs, delivered to the political committee by Lajos Czinege.
141 Povolný, 2018. 107.
142 HL, MN 1968—Zala, 4. doboz (box), 8. ő. e.
143 The withdrawal of Soviet troops did not go smoothly. Marshall Jakubovski did not reveal when the Soviet units would leave the territory of Czechoslovakia, in spite of being repeatedly asked. Minister of Defence, Dzúr, sent him a letter on the 4th of July, and Vice President Černík sent another one on the 11th of July, but both letters remained unanswered. Černík also asked Brezhnev about the presence of Soviet units in Czechoslovakia during the meeting in Čierna nad Tisou between the 27th of July and the 2nd of August (Povolný, 2018. 108–109).

Czechoslovak leadership "does not analyse the situation, underestimates the danger", Dubček "refuses a strict counterattack saying the time has not come yet." The attack target was also Ludvík Vaculík's manifesto "The two thousand words/Dvetisíc slov/",[144] published on June 27 and refused also by Kádár.

"The roads are divided ..." Preparation of the occupation

The political manifesto *The Two Thousand Words* (/Dvetisíc slov/) was a good excuse for the Soviets to postpone the troop withdrawal from Czechoslovakia and to announce the summit of the "six parties". This time, they chose Warsaw for the meeting. The leadership of KSČ with Dubček at its head attended the meeting in Dresden (March 23), they did not get an invite from Moscow (May 6) and they did not even want to go to Warsaw. Instead, Dubček met Kádár in Komárno on the 23rd of July, one day before the meeting in Warsaw.[145] In the early morning hours of the next day, János Kádár and Jenő Fock left for Warsaw. Deputy Foreign Minister Károly Erdélyi and Major-General Ferenc Sebestyén were in the delegation as well.[146] Sebestyén's presence serves as a proof that the Hungarian delegation counted on the fact that in Warsaw, the debates were to touch also military issues. This fact is confirmed also by the political committee MSZMP, on July 12. It is evident from the speeches of those present that they were conscious of what it was really about. The members of the political bureau agreed with the Hungarian delegation being an intermediary. During the debate, there were announcements: "a military intervention

---

144 Ludvík Vaculík: Dva tisíce slov—The Two Thousand Words. *Literární noviny*. July 27, 1968.
145 Vasiľ Biľak and Štefan Sádovský travelled on the same day to Balatonliga. Unfortunately, there are neither Hungarian, nor Slovak nor Czech sources to prove who they met or what they talked about. There is only one entry on their arrival: MNL OL, XIX-J-1-u, Miniszter és miniszterhelyettesi iratok (Erdélyi Károly iratai) (Documents of the Minister and Deputy Minister Károly Erdélyi) 17. doboz (box). We believe the Czechoslovak hosts met with Kádár in Balatonliga. Biľak was the only member of ÚV KSČ who supported the participation on the Warsaw meeting. See: Jašek, 2017. Biľak met with György Aczél on the 6th July and told him "The Two Thousand Words" represented the line of what was bearable and after that "the party should have intervened against the enemies" even using administrative means. MNL OL, M-KS 288. f. 47/743. ő. e.
146 MNL OL, XIX-J-1-u, Miniszter és miniszterhelyettesi iratok (Erdélyi Károly iratai) (Documents of the Minister and Deputy Minister Károly Erdélyi), 17. doboz (box).

can cause damage", "let us not support a military action", "let us keep the position we held until now" and "a military intervention is a mistake".[147]

Also Kádár had to talk with Dubček, since until then he had acted in defence of Czechoslovak events before the other Socialist parties and now he came to the conclusion that Dubček betrayed him. During the one to one meeting, Kádár was nervous because he was conscious of the fact that in Warsaw he had been the only one to defend Czechoslovakia and this was no longer defensible. The allegation that the KSČ leadership wanted to keep the friendly relations with the Soviet Union also in the future would not sound true. He also could not defend *"The Two Thousand Words"* in the name of Dubček, he knew exactly how the military training Šumava went and he also got the information the Soviets were preparing a sequel. He received a letter which contained a sharp condemn of the Czechoslovak reform processes and this also contained a passage on a possible "offer of help". Kádár participated in the preparations for the meeting in Warsaw and commented on this document. He was also in Moscow and—if he had doubted the Soviets' intentions before—these doubts definitely disappeared after this meeting. He was aware that the primary aim of the Warsaw debate was to put a choice before Dubček and his leadership: if they participate, it will be a clear signal that they abandon the reformist wing; if not, the Soviet leadership will no longer be behind them.

Kádár considered it crucial to convince KSČ leadership of its participation in the Warsaw meeting. Dubček was at times aware that the event could end in tragedy, at least it looks like that from the reasons he gave for his absence in Warsaw. In his opinion, it was impossible to adopt a single position "until they did not clear with the particular parties (East Germany, Bulgaria) if it was counterrevolution?". "Because military orders can be debated and decided this way." At the same time he complained to Kádár that the Soviet soldiers were still in Czechoslovakia and it was not known when they would leave.[148]

Kádár then informed Dubček on the situation:

> The refusal to participate in a multilateral meeting is the biggest mistake you have done since January. This fact has changed the relations between six parties. This is a serious situation and nobody can say what will come next. (...) If the KSČ leadership refuses the participation in multilateral debate, then this is our

---

147   MNL OL, M-KS 288. f. 47/743. ő. e.
148   MNL OL, M-KS 288. f. 47/743. ő. e.

crossroads. Which way will you go and who with? If you do not come to Warsaw, you will negate your previous positions and at the same time put also the Hungarian party to an uneasy situation.[149]

In Kádár's words, this comment was not expected by Dubček and Černík: 'At that moment they probably realized where this has come to. This phase of the conversation broke them, they started to cry.[150] In such psychical state they declared that all doors have been slammed on them.'[151] Dubček asked what was the reason it was so urgent that the leaders met and Kádár answered: "Don't you know your partners."[152]

15th July in Warsaw really meant the crossroads and door slamming. Also Kádár gave up on his previous positions. However, it was not easy. The Hungarian leading representative mentioned in his speech all possible statements from the meetings in Dresden and Moscow, but he added that the situation was now much worse than before. The crucial question remained, if there was counterrevolution in Czechoslovakia. In Kádár's opinion not yet, but it would not take long to come. Therefore, he suggested keeping the political fight.[153]

After Kádár spoke Ulbricht and attacked the Hungarian leader:

> 'I was surprised at the analysis presented by comrade Kádár. It is evident, comrade Kádár, that this is not only about Czechoslovakia (…) It is about counterrevolutionary powers. (…) I am not sure, comrade Kádár, do you not see it? Do you not see that the imperialism will strike in Hungary next? It is obvious that the imperialist centres develop their activities in Hungarian intellectual circles."[154]

---

149 MNL OL, M-KS 288. f. 5/462. ő. e.
150 Kádár's speech in the political committee MSZMP 15th July 1968, See: MNL OL, M-KS 288. f. 5/462. ő. e. Kádár informed on the psychical state of the Czechoslovak leading representatives two days later during the meeting in Warsaw: "They became aware of how serious the situation is only during the talks and that broke them. Especially Dubček who could not speak a word. Both cried." Garlicki—Paczkowski, 1995. Quotation in Hungarian: Földes, 2015. II. 281.
151 In the inform for ÚV KSČ this sentence was as follows: "If they call the meeting for tomorrow morning, that will cause the doors to shut before our position." Vondrová—Navrátil, 1995. 304.
152 The document states: "Nieznáte partnery?" Vondrová—Navrátil, 1995. 303. According to the memoirs of Zdeněk Mlynář, Kádár asked this question three days before the military intervention, on the 17th of August, 1968: "Tell me, do you seriously not know who you are dealing with?" (Mlynář, 1989. 147.) According to other available sources, this question appeared already on the 23rd of July before the Warsaw meeting.
153 Földes, 2015. II. 282–285.
154 Ibid., 285–286.

During the debate, Brezhnev came to the following conclusion: "I have the right to evaluate this development of events as representing a direct threat on the position of socialism in the world and our countries. If we oppose to it, it cannot be considered mixing in the internal affairs of Czechoslovakia."[155] Brezhnev did not say it explicitly, but following his thoughts, it was logical to say that if he evaluates the situation as "dangerous to the socialist movement", there is only one solution left for the Soviet Union ...

Kádár was not only left alone with his position but he also had to face personal attacks. Therefore, he asked to speak again and said: "As far as the evaluation of the Soviet comrades and the consequences of this evaluation, I completely agree with them and we are ready to participate in any joint action."[156] Kádár resigned on his previous position and opposed to what he said on 12th July, he agreed Hungary to join in the "common action."[157]

In spite of the fact that Kádár resigned during the meeting of the 'five' on his previous positions, he still believed he could by all means at his disposal prevent a military intervention. It was not acceptable from the point of view of Hungarian reforms if there was a conservative turn in the socialist group. After the debate, Kádár in his conversation with Brezhnev and Kosygin carefully reminded the Soviet leadership of their historical responsibility and of the necessity to use even the smallest opportunity for a peace solution. What he did not dare say before the whole gathering, he expressed in the conversation between six eyes: the situation does not remind the year 1956 in Hungary, but in Poland,[158] therefore, it should be considered to call a Soviet-Czechoslovak meeting.[159] Brezhnev promised to do so.

---

155 Ibid., 300–301.
156 Ibid., 302.
157 The representatives of five parties made a letter addressed to ÚV KSČ that was also published in the Hungarian press. *Népszabadság*, July 18, 1968.
158 This was also a radical turn in Kádár's position because he himself had compared the Czechoslovak development to the Hungarian event in 1956, better say to what happened before 23rd October. Now he had to use the argument against a military intervention so he used the parallel with the Polish situation in 1956. He also said he did not believe it was a counterrevolution.
159 MNL OL, M-KS 288.f. 5/462. ő. e.

On July 10, some days before the meeting, Major-General Ivan Tutarinov[160] delivered to the Hungarian Minister of Defence Lajos Czinege a message from the Soviet Minister of Defence Grechko—that another military training was to take place in the territory of Czechoslovakia. They counted on the participation of *three Hungarian divisions*: in the first phase, they needed two divisions, in the next phase, one. The military training was to take place in July. Tutarinov referred to a telephone agreement between Brezhnev and Kádár. The Hungarian Minister of Defence answered on the same day to Grechko saying it was a misunderstanding since Kádár did not know about this request. The Soviet military command spoke again one week after the meeting of *'the five'* in Warsaw. On July 22 at 14:00 hours, Tutarinov informed the Staff General and Deputy Minister of Defence Károly Csémi: "Comrade Grechko requests you send at least one division for the training and if that is not possible, a smaller military unit is enough."[161]

The second possibility was approved in a closed meeting of the political committee MSZMP on 23rd July 1968. At the same time a resolution was approved within which "we will support their proposal during the *planning* of the military training: we will send a *smaller* military unit."[162] The Hungarian military command sent its decision to the Soviets that the Hungarian party would send a smaller division for the military training. It was also questionable if the Hungarians participate already in the initial phase or later.

The fact that it was not merely a military training is confirmed by Staff General Károly Csémi on 24th July 1968. The political aim of the training was much harsher than in the case of the training Šumava. "To offer help to the Czechoslovak people in their fight against counterrevolution. (…) If the military units are loyal, we will not hurt them, but if they show resistance, we will take action. (…) Depending on the activities of the Czechoslovak People's Army, there can be an armed encounter."

---

160 Deputy Head of the Armed Forces of the Warsaw Pact in Hungary. Tutarinov was a general in the defeat of the Hungarian revolution in 1956 within the military operation Storm (Vihar).
161 HL, MN 1968—Zala, 4. doboz. 8. ő. e.
162 MNL OL, M-KS 288. f. 5. cs. 464. ő. e.

The Soviets did not inform on the exact date of the military training but it was expected at any time after 26–27 July.[163]

The Hungarian command chose for the training the 8th Motor rifle division of Zalaegerszeg. According to the military operation plans, the division was to take over the territory of ten thousand square kilometres on the first day of the occupation until 14:00 hours, occupy ten positions of local garrison.[164] Mobilisation in Hungary started five days later (a military training with the cover name "Zala") and several days later also in Poland (cover name "Cloudy summer—1968"/"Zamračené leto—1968"). However, after the meetings in Čierna nad Tisou and Bratislava (August 2), the order to stop the mobilisation came.[165] The reason of such change was perhaps the fact that even in Moscow there were leading representatives who did not agree with a military occupation of Czechoslovakia.[166] There was no final decision yet on a political level.

A flash of light

Czechoslovak leadership was aware of the dangers. For this reason another Soviet-Czechoslovak bilateral meeting took place in Čierna nad Tisou from July 29 to August 1. Following this, a similar set of events happened as after the Moscow meeting—on August 6, the representatives of six parties met in Bratislava (East Germany, Hungary, Poland, Soviet Union and Czechoslovakia) and signed a joint agreement. The supporters of the Soviet intervention needed a legitimate base for their planned step.

János Kádár visited Brezhnev in Yalta on August 12–15. On August 13, Brezhnev and Dubček talked on the telephone. The Secretary General of the CPSU asked Dubček a single question: what was to be decided on the meeting of ÚV KSČ? He wanted to know if the Central Committee would take full control over the mass media, for example if it would interfere in cadre matters. Dubček avoided a direct answer and asked for time to discuss these issues during the next plenary of the Central Committee. Brezhnev accused Dubček of swindling the leadership of the CPSU and

---

163 János Kádár and Béla Biszka received Csémi's report. HL, MN 1968—Zala, 4. doboz. 8. ő. e.
164 *"Zala" 1968.*, 2012.
165 Ibid., 31.
166 Pihoja, 1998. 22–23.

said the Chairmanship of the Central Committee had no power. Dubček did not offer any clear answers and stated he had nothing to add. "If you think we swindle", he said "undergo the steps you consider convenient. That is your business."[167] The Soviet leader became convinced that Dubček would not follow the decisions from the meetings in Čierna nad Tisou and in Bratislava.

Kádár definitely knew about the telephone conversation, because on the 15th of August, after his return from Yalta, he sent a written invitation for a meeting to Dubček to debate the current issues. Dubček in his reply suggested they meet on August 17 at 15:00 hours in Komárno. Kádár informed Brezhnev and promised to inform him on the outcome of the talk. At the same time, Kádár received a message from Brezhnev on the 17th of August in which he asked "in relation with the complications in Czechoslovakia, comrade Kádár to come to Moscow on 18th August at 10:00 hours."[168] During the meeting with Dubček, Kádár knew there was to be another meeting of 'the five'. For this reason, Kádár, Erdély, Dubček and Černík met in Komárno in secret.

Kádár did not mention the planned Moscow meeting nor the occupation plan during the meeting. However, from what he did reveal Dubček must have understood that Kádár adopted a decisive position. He was much more critical and from the overall context it was clear what direction the events developing in. He described the meeting in Bratislava as a historic one: 'because we not only achieved something but we also impeded certain things'[169]—referring to the fact that if there was no joint agreement, the military intervention would already have happened.[170]

---

167 See: *Chekhoslovatskiy krizis 1967–1969 gg.*, 2010. 851–861.
168 MNL OL, M-KS 288. f. 47/743. ő. e. 190–191, 195–197. The decision fell in the meeting of the Political Committee ÚV KSSS. See: *Chekhoslovatskiy krizis 1967–1969 gg.*, 2010. 184.
169 Handwritten notes of Károly Erdélyi are available from this debate (published: Földes, 2015. I. 308–325.). Kádár informed on it also in a closed meeting of the Central Committee MSZMP and the Council of Ministers on 23rd August 1968. (MNL OL, M-KS 288. f. 4/94. ő. e. 9–10.).
170 Dubček and his companions did not understand Kádár. His inform for the Chairmanship of ÚV KSČ proves this. They do not quote Kádár directly, but rather in a neutral form: "The leadership of MSZMP evaluates the meeting in Bratislava and its importance as a positive one." NA ČR, KSČ-ÚV-02/1. sv. 81. a.j. 126/kinf1.

After that, the two leading representatives of the party discussed who had made a mistake "before Warsaw": KSČ or "the five"? Dubček insisted it had not been them, but the fault was in the Warsaw meeting and "the letter from Warsaw". Kádár disagreed. On the first sight it resembled a superficial debate but in fact Kádár wanted to make sure how serious was the Czechoslovak leadership about the agreement from Bratislava. Was it only an obligatory compromise or did the Dubček group finally understand it had not been a correct decision not to join 'the five' before the meeting in Warsaw. And is Dubček serious about his return to the "right path"? "It is not irrelevant what they think because they can separate us again", said Kádár.[171]—He tried to say the conflict went on.

Kádár considered the meeting in Warsaw a challenge. He had to change his position and retreat. He was obliged to adopt a position he did not agree with. He promised before the gathered that he "will join in all joint actions". Dubček defended the absence of the KSČ leadership on the Warsaw meeting also on the meeting on 17th August. It is therefore not a coincidence that during the conversation Kádár shouted: "Where are our rights? We only assist …"—meaning the MSZMP leadership participated in all meetings on Czechoslovak issues, even in Bratislava, although they did not know what to expect and what was to be debated. He could not explain to Dubček the importance of the debate in Bratislava, which consisted precisely in the fact that thanks to them he postponed the plan of military intervention that had been decided already in Warsaw. Kádár felt relieved at least for a while because everything proved that so far he did not have to fulfil his promise given in Warsaw about "the participation in joint actions".

Kádár criticized especially the fact that the Chairmanship of ÚV KSČ did not summon a meeting immediately after the Bratislava debate, where the controversial point would be talked. "In your place, the Chairmanship of our party would have summoned a five day meeting"—he said. Kádár eventually lost balance: "I have not received neither rubles nor zlotys. Simply, there are things that need to be considered. Eight months have passed and one gets the feeling you lack courage to set clear borders. Everything goes as if you were dropping sand through your fingers."[172] "I

---

171 All quotes from notes of Károly Erdélyi. Földes, 2015. II. 312–313.
172 All quotes from notes of Károly Erdélyi. Földes, 2015. II. 312–313.

believed you from the first day!" Dubček replied: "If you do not give us two weeks, find another first secretary!"[173][...]

"Tell me, what do I do?" Kádár: "Prepare a congress and take all practical steps!"[174] ÚV KSČ however, did not have two weeks to act.

Occupation

On the next day, Kádár travelled to Moscow, where Brezhnev informed him: Czechoslovakia will be occupied by the armies of the member states of the Warsaw Pact.[175] On August 20, 1968, at 23:00 hours, the operation Danube/Dunaj began under the command of the Deputy Minister of Defence of the Soviet Union, Jurij Pavlovski, the armed forces of the Soviet Union, Poland, Bulgaria and Hungary crossed the border on 18 places and entered the territory of Czechoslovakia. Within the Warsaw Pact, this was how the only and at the same time the last sharp deployment of the Hungarian People's Army performed in the period after WW2.

From the 18 places to pass the state border, three were assigned to the Hungarian division that entered the country in southwest Slovakia with a large population of Hungarian nationality. From the military operation Zala, some ten thousand soldiers participated in the occupation of Czechoslovakia and together 160 military vehicles of the types T-54/A (93), T-55 (24) a T-55/A (43). From Poland, the most vehement defenders of the occupation plan, the 2nd armada under the command of Florian Siwicki occupied a territory twice as large (20 thousand square metres), and the number of Polish soldiers considerably outnumbered the Hungarians (Polish historians estimate there were 20 thousand). Apart from that, 600 Polish tanks outnumbered the number of military vehicles of the Hungarian division.[176] Until August 25, 27 divisions participated in the invasion to Czechoslovakia (12 tank divisions, 13 motorized and 2 plane), 6300

---

173 Ibid 318. Dubček said the same as in the telephone conversation with Brezhnev on 13th August.
174 Ibid 320–321.
175 Kádár announced in his short speech that he had met Dubček on the previous day and their debate was rather unpleasant. He did not find out if Dubček was serious about the agreement from Bratislava. In spite of that, he insisted on a political agreement which would take place after the military intervention which all parties had agreed on. See: Vondrová—Navrátil, 1996. 203–204.
176 For this data, see: Kowalski, 1992. 18.

tanks, 2000 cannons, 550 combat and 250 transportation helicopters.[177] The number of soldiers is estimated at between 200,000 and 250,000. From the data it is evident that the participation of the Hungarian division was of symbolic character. When we consider that Hungary occupied a territory in which it could find the smallest resistance, we can say that the Hungarian participation on the occupation of Czechoslovakia did not have a large importance from the military point of view.[178]

This fact is proved also by the reports on the situation in which there are also an insignificant number of cases of violence against the Hungarian soldiers (one of them happened when a Czechoslovak truck pushed the vehicle of a Hungarian soldier off the road. The soldier was injured and he was treated for 8 days from these injuries).[179] Taking into consideration that until the end of 1968, the occupation had, on the side of the resistance, 137 fatalities and 500 seriously injured, it is evident that the Hungarian soldiers had not entered into "problematic territories".[180]

During the whole occupation—from the order number 001 of the Commander of 8th Infantry Division on the 29th of July until the complete retirement of the troops on the 30th of October, the Hungarian soldiers were not deployed in sharp combat. From the Hungarian division, four soldiers died, only one case occurring during a military action: one T-54 vehicle fell into the river Ipľa and the reserve officer in it died; another fatality was caused by heart thrombose; one person died as a consequence of "accident with a firearm" (one soldier accidentally shot another); and a fourth soldier died while on leave by committing suicide.[181]

Kádár talked about Hungarian foreign policy on October 24, at the time when the Hungarian army was leaving Czechoslovakia and he chose an unusual place for his speech—a factory for socks in Budapest: "The

---

177 Povolný, 2018. 356.
178 They did not have to count on large resistance because they could rely on the fact that in the territories with Hungarian population people would not attack on Hungarian soldiers. On the other hand, the population in Slovakia was less interested in Prague reformation processes therefore the events of occupation and normalization had a smaller response of the society. See: Pithart, 1993.
179 *"Zala" 1968.*, 2012. 89.
180 Data available online: http://www.ustrcr.cz/cs/obeti-okupace (last date visited 30th August 2018). In the territory occupied by the Hungarian army, there were four Czechoslovak victims until 8th September.
181 *"Zala" 1968.*, 2012. 36., 37., 57., 97.

basic thesis of our foreign policy is that we cooperate with the Soviet Union, the first socialist country and with the Communist Party of the Soviet Union." He added that this happens also when "the opinions of the socialist countries differ or are contradictory or opposed to each other."[182] A grotesque historical parallel is represented by the fact that in Autumn 1956 also the Czechoslovak leadership rationalised their military position in relation to the Hungarian revolution with a similar foreign policy thesis: "With the Soviet Union forever and never otherwise!" After 1956 as well as after 1968, it became clear that adjusting to the aims of an empire does not allow the subordinate countries to lead autonomous policy. János Kádár could not even defend Hungarian reforms.

---

182   *Népszabadság,* October 25, 1968.

07
The Communist Authorities and Polish Society in the Face of the Prague Spring and the Intervention in Czechoslovakia in 1968

Mirosław Szumiło
Maria Curie-Sklodowska University, Lublin
The Institute of National Remembrance, Warsaw

The position of Władysław Gomułka and the authorities of the People's Republic of Poland (PRP) towards the "Prague Spring" and the intervention of the Warsaw Pact in Czechoslovakia has already been discussed in numerous publications.[183] However, the reactions of Polish society are not

---

183 Paweł Machcewicz, "K čertu se suverenitou". Władysław Gomułka a Pražske jaro ["To hell with sovereignty". Władysław Gomułka and the Prague spring], in: Petr Blažek, Łukasz Kamiński and Rudolf Vévoda, eds., Polsko a Československo w roce 1968. Sborník příspěvků z mezinárodní vědecké konference [Poland and Czechoslovakia in 1968. Proceedings of an international scientific conference] (Praha: Ústav pro soudobe dejiny AV ČR, Dokořan, 2006); Łukasz Kamiński, Polská sjednocená dělnická strana a Pražske jaro [Polish United Workers' Party and Prague Spring], in: Petr Blažek, Łukasz Kamiński and Rudolf Vévoda, eds., Polsko a Československo w roce 1968. Sborník příspěvků z mezinárodní vědecké konference (Praha: Ústav pro soudobe dejiny AV ČR, Dokořan, 2006); Jerzy Eisler, *Polski rok 1968* [Polish year 1968] (Warszawa: Instytut Pamięci Narodowej, 2006); Leszek Pajórek, *Polska a "Praska Wiosna". Udział Wojska Polskiego w interwencji zbrojnej w Czechosłowacji w 1968 roku* [Poland and the "Prague Spring". The participation of the Polish Army in the military intervention in Czechoslovakia in 1968] (Warszawa: Egros, 1998); Leszek Pajórek, Polsko a pražske jaro 1968 [Poland and the Prague Spring 1968], *Soudobé dějiny*, 1996, č. 2–3, 221–263; Lech Kowalski, *Kryptonim "Dunaj". Udział wojsk polskich w interwencji zbrojnej w Czechosłowacji w 1968 roku* [Code name "Danube". The participation of Polish troops in the military intervention in Czechoslovakia in 1968] (Warszawa: Książka i Wiedza, 1992); Łukasz Kamiński, Od kryzysu do kryzysu. Przyczynek do dziejów stosunków PRL-CSRS w latach 1956–1970, [From crisis to crisis. Contribution to the history of PRL-CSRS relations in the years 1956–1970], in: Krzysztof Ruchniewicz, Bożena Szaynok, Jakub Tyszkiewicz, eds., *Między Październikiem a Grudniem. Polityka zagraniczna doby Gomułki* [Between October and December. Foreign policy of the Gomułka era] (Toruń: Wydawnictwo Adam Marszałek, 2005), 121–135.

so well known.[184] Therefore, in this article I shall focus on the latter issue, presenting briefly the position of the leadership of the Polish United Workers' Party (PUWP) and the propaganda campaign in the press.

The then First Secretary of the Central Committee (CC) of the PUWP, Władysław Gomułka, had become the leader of the Party and the state as a result of the period of "thaw" and transformations in Poland in 1956. He proclaimed the slogan of "the Polish road to Socialism", and was seen as a Party reformer, like Dubček twelve years later in Czechoslovakia. However, the stage of the liberalization of the system ended after just one year. Gomułka consolidated the power of the system, restored strict censorship in the media, and gradually increased control over all areas of social life. In 1968, the leader of the PUWP was already completely set in his ways and incapable of any reform.

The Czechoslovakian Ambassador to Warsaw, Antonín Gregor, reported that, from the time when Alexander Dubček took the position of the First Secretary of the Communist Party of Czechoslovakia (CPCz), the PUWP leadership had been observing the changes in the neighbouring state with growing attention and greater and greater worry.[185] The editor-in-chief of 'Polityka' weekly, Mieczysław Rakowski, noted in his diary on

---

184 About Polish protests in 1968 wrote Łukasz Kamiński (Łukasz Kamiński, Ręce precz od Czechów! Polacy wobec inwazji na Czechosłowację w 1968 r. [Hands off the Czechs! Poles on the invasion of Czechoslovakia in 1968], *Więź*, 2004, no 7, 80–91; Łukasz Kamiński, Polská společnost a invaze vojsk Varšavské smlouvy do Československa [Polish society and the invasion of Warsaw Pact troops into Czechoslovakia], In: Petr Blažek, eds., *Opozice a odpor proti komunistickému režimu v Československu 1968–1989* [Opposition and resistance to the communist regime in Czechoslovakia 1968–1989] (Praha: Ústav Českých Dějin FF UK, Dokořan, 2005), 270–289) and Grzegorz Majchrzak (Grzegorz Majchrzak, Nie tylko Siwiec. Polskie protesty przeciwko interwencji w Czechosłowacji [Not only Siwiec. Polish protests against the intervention in Czechoslovakia], In: Tomasz Kozłowski and Jan Olaszek, eds., *Opozycja i opór społeczny w Polsce po 1956 roku* [Opposition and social resistance in Poland after 1956] (Warszawa: Instytut Pamięci Narodowej, 2014), vol. 2, 97–112; Grzegorz Majchrzak, Poľské občianske protesty proti intervencii v Československu z pohľadu bezpečnostných dokumentov [Polish civil protests against intervention in Czechoslovakia from the point of view of security documents], *Pamäť národa*, 2018, Part 2, 39–56).
185 František Janaček, Jan Moravec, Leden 1968 a spor o jeho smysl [January 1968 and a dispute over its meaning], In: Václav Kural, eds., *Československo 1968: Obrodný proces* [Czechoslovakia 1968: Revival process] (Praha: Parta, 1993), 32–33.

January 17, 1968 that part of the Polish leadership were scared by the events in Czechoslovakia.[186]

The first meeting between Dubček and the Polish leader took place in Ostrava, on February 7, 1968. Dubček informed Gomułka about the reasons for dismissing Antonín Novotny from the position of the First Secretary of the CPCz, emphasized his wish for continuing the earlier internal and international politics of Czechoslovakia and gave a brief presentation of the planned reforms. However, Gomułka did not hide his worry concerning the developments in Czechoslovakia. He warned Dubček against a radical reappraisal of Stalinism, which could be exploited by "revisionists" and threatened the dismantling of the socialism. He openly said that "anti-Socialist" forces in Czechoslovakia could activate "hostile elements" in Poland into action. As an example of such bad influences, Gomułka gave writers: "Our writers are now quoting the processes taking place in your writers' milieu".[187]

When judging Gomułka's stand in Ostrava, we should remember that a few days earlier (on January 30) Warsaw witnessed a demonstration against banning further performances of "Dziady" (authored by Adam Mickiewicz) at the National Theatre. There was growing dissatisfaction in student and intelligentsia circles. Events that in a way confirmed Gomułka's fears took place a month later. On 8 March 1968, students' protests broke out in Warsaw, and then spread to a dozen cities in Poland. There were strikes, demonstrations in the streets, fights with the 'militia'—with mass participation not only by the student youth, but also by young workers.

During those protests, slogans of democratization and freedom of speech were accompanied by expressions of solidarity with the Czechs and Slovaks. On March 9, during the demonstration in front of the Centre for Czechoslovakian Culture, the participants chanted: "Bravo Czechs!" and "The whole of Poland is waiting for her Dubček".[188] The latter cry was also

---

186 Mieczysław Rakowski, Dzienniki polityczne 1967–1968 [Political diaries 1967–1968] (Warszawa: Iskry, 1999), 113.
187 Protokół z rozmowy I sekretarza KC PZPR Władysława Gomułki z I sekretarzem KC KPCZ Aleksandrem Dubczekiem [Minutes of a conversation the First Secretary of CC PUWP Władysław Gomułka with the First Secretary of CC KPCz Alexander Dubček], In: Andrzej Garlicki, Andrzej Paczkowski, eds., Zaciskanie pętli. Tajne dokumenty dotyczące Czechosłowacji 1968 [Tightening the loops. Secret documents on Czechoslovakia 1968] (Warszawa: Wydawnictwo Sejmowe, 1995), 17–25; Paweł Machcewicz, "K čertu se suverenitou". Władysław Gomułka a Pražske jaro, 83–86.
188 Jerzy Eisler, Polski rok 1968, 268.

raised two days later, in front of the building housing the Central Committee of the PUWP.[189] Things were similar in other cities as well. On March 12, during a night youth march in Częstochowa, one could hear, among others, the cries "Long live Czechoslovakia!" and "Long live Dubček!".[190] In the declaration adopted by students in Poznań on March 13, the authors wrote: "We show solidarity with and greet the heroic students of brotherly Czechoslovakia." Similar leaflets were distributed in Lodz and Wroclaw.[191]

These expressions of solidarity met with a response from the other side. Czechoslovak people were following the situation in Poland with great interest. Already, a few days after the onset of student protests, the protests became the subject of detailed comments in the press and on the radio. Expulsions of students and lecturers from universities, attacks on writers and artists and a primitive anti-Semitic campaign were described with a high degree of objectivity.[192] Letters were sent from Czechoslovakia to Poland with touching expressions of solidarity with Polish students and intellectuals. On March 12, 1968, students from the Faculty of Philosophy at the Charles University in Prague sent a letter "to all Warsaw students". The students expressed, in that letter, their support for the fight for the democratization of public life and for respecting individual freedoms and elementary human rights. The letter was intercepted and confiscated by the Polish Security Service (Służba Bezpieczeństwa—SB)[193].

---

189 Ibidem, 534.
190 Jarosław Neja, Katowice i województwo katowickie [Katowice and the Katowice Province], In: Konrad Rokicki, Sławomir Stępień, eds., *Oblicza Marca 1968* [Faces of March 1968] (Warszawa: Instytut Pamięci Narodowej, 2004), 105.
191 Jerzy Eisler, Vliv Pražského jara na polský Březen [The influence of the Prague Spring on Polish March], in: Petr Blažek, Łukasz Kamiński and Rudolf Vévoda, eds., Polsko a Československo w roce 1968. Sborník příspěvků z mezinárodní vědecké konference [Poland and Czechoslovakia in 1968. Proceedings of an international scientific conference] (Praha: Ústav pro soudobe dejiny AV ČR, Dokořan, 2006), 33–44.
192 Petr Blažek, "Všechno dostane jiný směr". Vliv polského Března na Pražské jaro ["Everything gets a different direction." The influence of the Polish March on the Prague Spring], In: Petr Blažek, Łukasz Kamiński and Rudolf Vévoda, eds., Polsko a Československo w roce 1968. Sborník příspěvků z mezinárodní vědecké konference (Praha: Ústav pro soudobe dejiny AV ČR, Dokořan, 2006), 48–50.
193 Jerzy Eisler, Vliv Pražského jara na polský Březen, p. 31. Further on that subject, see Maciej Górny, Wydarzenia marcowe w opinii czechosłowackiej [March events in the opinion of Czechoslovakia], In: Marcin Kula, Piotr Osęka, Marcin Zaremba, eds.,

The stand of Czechoslovak journalists raised extensive concerns in the PUWP leadership, especially those Poles who had acquired their knowledge of events in their country by listening to "Radio Praha". This is why the Polish Ministry of Foreign Affairs (MSZ) submitted official notes to Ambassador Gregor several times, protesting against the Czechoslovak media exposing and commenting on the situation existing in Poland.[194] At the order of the PUWP leadership, the Polish Security Service covered, with their operational control, contacts between citizens of Poland and Czechoslovakia (mainly those from "revisionist and Zionist milieus" as well as scientists, journalists and employees of cultural institutions). Furthermore, the border traffic between both countries was limited and strictly controlled.[195] Solidarity with reform in Czechoslovakia, expressed by the protesting Polish students, and the response from the other side, had a great impact on Władysław Gomułka's attitude towards the Prague Spring.

During the aforementioned meeting in Ostrava, Gomułka did not yet resort to open criticism of the Czechoslovak leadership's actions. However, after the onset of student protests in Poland, the dominant tone of his speeches at the meeting of Communist party leaders in Dresden on March 23 was much sharper. "I was sorry to note that the sharpest criticism of our actions came from Gomułka", recalled Dubček.[196] Gomułka compared the ongoing events in Poland and Czechoslovakia, referring also to the experiences of 1956 in Poland and in Hungary. He spoke of a widespread "revisionist" conspiracy (represented by writers and intellectuals and directed by emigration milieus and foreign intelligence services). He called for "barring the path of counter-revolution", stating that the internal affairs of

---

Marzec 1968. Trzydzieści lat później, Vol. 1, [March 1968. Thirty years later] (Warszawa: Wydawnictwo Naukowe PWN, 1998), 206–218.
194 Jerzy Eisler, Vliv Pražského jara na polský Březen, 27–28.
195 Grzegorz Majchrzak, Służba Bezpieczeństwa PRL a Praska Wiosna [The Security Service of the People's Republic of Poland and the Prague Spring], In: Jerzy Eisler et al., eds., Aparat bezpieczeństwa, propaganda a Praska Wiosna. Zbiór materiałów z konferencji międzynarodowej Praga, 7–9 września 2008 r. [Security apparatus, propaganda and the Prague Spring. Collection of materials from the international conference Prague, September 7–9, 2008] (Praha: Ústav pro studium totalitních režimů, 2009), 85–86.
196 Alexander Dubček, Naděje umírá poslední. Vlastní životopis Alexandra Dubčeka [Hope dies last. Own biography of Alexander Dubček], (Praha: Svoboda-Libertas, 1993), 152.

Czechoslovakia had become the affairs "of the whole Socialist camp".[197] A few days later, during the meeting of the first secretaries of the voivodeship committees of the PUWP in Warsaw, Gomułka recognized the loss of control over mass media by the CPCz leadership as a very dangerous development. At the same time, he warned that the West aimed to exploit the events in Czechoslovakia in order to change the balance of power in Europe: "The enemy is banking on breaking down the Socialist camp, is staking on wresting Czechoslovakia out of the Socialist camp".[198]

Over the following weeks, Gomułka followed the events in Czechoslovakia with increasing attention and worry. On 16 April 1968, the Soviet Ambassador to Warsaw, Avierkij Aristov, informed Moscow that Gomułka had expressed the opinion about the necessity for "immediate intervention", since, in Poland, "very many people would like to repeat what is happening in Czechoslovakia".[199] On 19 April, Gomułka met the Commander-in-Chief of the Warsaw Pact's United Military Forces, Marshal Ivan Yakubovsky. Then, he expressed the opinion that the Soviet army should enter Czechoslovakia to protect the country from aggression by the Federal Republic of Germany (FRG).[200]

When speaking at the meeting of the leaders of five Communist parties in Moscow on May 6 1968, Gomułka formulated his own vision of a Czechoslovak "counter-revolution", which was, according to him, "a counter-revolution of a new type". In opposition to Hungary in 1956, when the enemies went out on the streets with weapons, this time it was happening in a peaceful way—under the aegis of improving Socialism. In his opinion, this was leading to gradual transformation "of the socialist

---

197 Stenographic Account of the Dresden Meeting, March 22, 1968 (Excerpts), In: Jaromír Navrátil, Antonín Benčík, Václav Kural, Marie Michálková, Jitka Vondrová, eds., *The Prague Spring 1968* (Budapest: CEU Press, 1998), 67.

198 Fragment wystąpienia Władysława Gomułki na naradzie pierwszych sekretarzy KW PZPR dotyczący spotkania w Dreźnie [Fragment of Władysław Gomułka's speech at the debate of the First Secretaries of VC PUWP regarding the meeting in Dresden], Warsaw, 26 March 1968, In: *Zaciskanie pętli. Tajne dokumenty dotyczące Czechosłowacji 1968*, 63–64, 74–75.

199 Cable to Moscow from Soviet Ambassador to Warsaw Averki Aristov Regarding Wladyslaw Gomulka's Views on the Situation in Czechoslovakia, April 16, 1968, In: *The Prague Spring 1968*, 103.

200 Leszek Pajórek, *Polska a "Praska Wiosna". Udział Wojska Polskiego w interwencji zbrojnej w Czechosłowacji w 1968 roku*, 96.

state" into a "bourgeois type" of republic. He charged the CPCz leadership with "breaking the unity of the Socialist block", which was exploited by the Western states, especially by the FRG. He reminded them that the western borders of Poland were not guaranteed by a peace treaty, and that the Germans were all the time striving to change them.[201]

All this indicates that Gomułka, together with other members of the PUWP leadership, really feared that Czechoslovakia would leave the Warsaw Pact. In his opinion, this could bring about a weakening of the Communist block of states, absorption of the GDR by the FRG, and a threat to the western borders of Poland.[202] Hence, it is no surprise that, from Gomułka's point of view, the best solution to the Czechoslovak problem was the incursion of Warsaw Pact armies into the territory of Czechoslovakia. Gomułka personally tried to persuade Brezhnev of this. During the debate of the leaders of Communist countries in Warsaw on July 14–15, 1968, he was calling for intervention.[203]

The armed intervention in Czechoslovakia, which began in the night of August 20/21, 1968, involved participation by the 2nd Army of the Polish Armed Forces, numbering close to thirty thousand soldiers, 750 tanks and 592 armed transporters. Polish troops occupied the territory of Eastern Czechoslovakia (Východočeský kraj) and a large part of the North Moravia (Severomoravský kraj). The command was located in Hradec Králové. The Polish Army stayed in Czechoslovak territory for 84 days.[204]

---

201 Záznam sovětské strany z porady "pětky" o "kontrarevoluční" situaci v Československu a opatřeních k jejímu řešení [Record of the Soviet party from the meeting of the "five" about the "counter-revolutionary" situation in Czechoslovakia and measures to solve it], In: Jitka Vondrová, Jaromír Navratil, eds., *Mezinárodní souvislosti československé krize. Prosinec 1967–červenec 1968* [International context of the Czechoslovak crisis. December 1967–July 1968] (Brno: Ústav pro soudobe dejiny AV ČR and Doplněk, 1995), 207.

202 Archiwum Akt Nowych [Archives of New Files] in Warsaw, Komitet Centralny PZPR [CC PUWP], XIA/37, Minutes of the First Secretary of CC PUWP Władysław Gomułka's conversation with President of Czechoslovakia Ludvík Svoboda, Warsaw, 01.09.1959, 154–155; Paweł Machcewicz, "K čertu se suverenitou". Władysław Gomułka a Pražske jaro, 92–94.

203 Ibid., 90–91, 94–95.

204 Paweł Piotrowski, Účast Polské armády na intervenci v Československu [Participation of the Polish army in intervention in Czechoslovakia], In: Petr Blažek, Łukasz Kamiński and Rudolf Vévoda, eds., Polsko a Československo w roce 1968. Sborník příspěvků z

At the same time, the Polish Security Service began a secret operation, "Podhale", under which they tried to recognize the situation and feeling in the area of Czechoslovakia, put the Czechs and Slovaks staying in the area of the Polish People's Republic under surveillance, and combatted "enemy propaganda" by censoring the correspondence and publications arriving in Poland from her southern neighbours. Most of those actions were terminated on September 16, 1968, but the operation continued from 1969 through to 1971. Secret collaborators sent reports on the ambience prevailing within the CPCz ranks and in the intelligentsia circles.[205]

After 21 August, Gomułka expressed the view that the intervention had been a necessity and a military success, but had turned out to be a failure on a political level. This was because the power had remained in the hands of the incumbent CPCz leadership, and the "sound forces in the Party" had proved too weak to take over the initiative. In the Autumn of 1968, Gomułka consistently demanded that Moscow should undertake more energetic actions in the fight with the "counter-revolution" and dismiss Dubček from his position.[206]

The PUWP leadership had already launched a propaganda campaign to convince both the Party's rank and file and the whole Polish society of the rightness of their position. As early as in May 1968, at the meetings of basic Party cells, special information was read out about the events at the southern neighbours, together with the protest note of the PUWP leadership and the PRP government against the "anti-Polish campaign" in the Czechoslovak media. The next letter to Party organizations was sent on July 28, in order to accustom members of the PUWP, and through them the whole of society, to the idea of armed intervention in Czechoslovakia. Then, on August 21, open meetings were held in all Party committees, at

---

mezinárodní vědecké konference (Praha: Ústav pro soudobe dejiny AV ČR, Dokořan, 2006), 146–152.

205 Grzegorz Majchrzak, Operace "Podhale" [Operation "Podhale"], In: Petr Blažek, Łukasz Kamiński and Rudolf Vévoda, eds., Polsko a Československo w roce 1968. Sborník příspěvků z mezinárodní vědecké konference (Praha: Ústav pro soudobe dejiny AV ČR, Dokořan, 2006), 156–171.

206 Protokół ze spotkania przywódców partii i rządów Bułgarii, NRD, Polski, Węgier i ZSRR [Minutes of the meeting of the Party and Government delegations of Bulgaria, GDR, Poland, Hungary and USSR], Moscow, 27.09.1968, In: *Zaciskanie pętli. Tajne dokumenty dotyczące Czechosłowacji 1968*, 208–244; Paweł Machcewicz, "K čertu se suverenitou". Władysław Gomułka a Pražske jaro, 97–98.

which a letter of the CC PUWP was read out, that justified the decision to apply force, and informed them that the incursion of Polish armed forces took place at the request of "Czechoslovak comrades".[207]

On August 21, a carefully planned propaganda offensive was launched, with the participation of the press, radio and television. A regular column titled "Around the events in Czechoslovakia" appeared in the central press organ of the Party, the "Trybuna Ludu" daily. The column informed the readers of the "anti-Polish actions of counter-revolutionaries and right-wing forces" and commented on the earlier attitude of the Czechoslovak media to the events of March 1968. The journalists wrote about anti-Polish demonstrations and marches in front of the Polish Embassy in Prague, and about the charges of anti-Semitism against the Poles on the part of "Zionist forces".[208]

An attempt to neutralize the sympathy of the Poles for reforms in Czechoslovakia was, for example, the article in the "Żołnierz Wolności" daily, informing the readers about the beating and mobbing of Polish women working in a Czechoslovakian factory by "extremist and counter-revolutionary elements".[209] The press also published information about displays of hostility towards Polish tourists by Czechs and, more rarely, Slovaks. The Polish correspondent in Prague, Zygmunt Broniarek, reported: "Rightist elements terrorize the population, assault foreign tourists. In some cases, Czech hoodlums smash the cars of Polish holiday makers, not caring that there are young children inside".[210]

Expressions of hostility were also encountered by Polish soldiers, who saw inscriptions such as "death to Warsaw" and "invaders". The reasons for this type of behaviour were not explained; instead, Czechs and

---

207 Łukasz Kamiński, Polská sjednocená dělnická strana a Pražske jaro, 104–109.
208 Mariusz Mazur, Nieoficjalne wzajemne stosunki Polaków, Czechów i Słowaków w okresie praskiej wiosny na łamach polskiej prasy [Unofficial mutual relations between Poles, Czechs and Slovaks in the Prague Spring period in the Polish press], In: Petr Blažek, Paweł Jaworski, Łukasz Kamiński, Rudolf Vévoda, eds., Między przymusową przyjaźnią a prawdziwą solidarnością. Czesi—Polacy—Słowacy 1938/39–1945–1989, [Between forced friendship and true solidarity. Czechs—Poles—Slovaks 1938/39–1945–1989] Part II, (Warszawa: Instytut Pamięci Narodowej, 2009), 193–195.
209 Antoni Kołaciński, Trudne drogi normalizacji [Difficult paths of normalization], Żołnierz Wolności, September 11, 1968.
210 Zygmunt Broniarek, Wśród polskich żołnierzy [Among Polish soldiers], Trybuna Ludu, August 28, 1968.

Slovaks were charged with nationalism. An accumulation of these type of reports, triggering the protest of each and every Polish reader, served as justification for the aggression. From this viewpoint, the invaders protected peace and Socialism, and, at the same time, defended the honour and dignity of the Poles.[211]

Most of the articles describing a negative attitude towards Poles date from the period between August 21 and 31, 1968. Starting from the first days of September, they appeared more and more rarely, and were replaced by texts showing positive interactions between Polish soldiers and citizens of Czechoslovakia. The need to justify the aggression gave way to convincing the readers of the stabilization and recovery of trust between the two nations. The Polish invaders were portrayed as disciplined, brave, devoted and dignified soldiers. The press wrote that they helped in fighting fires, rescued victims of accidents, assisted Czech farmers at harvest and worked in the fields.[212]

Such propaganda certainly influenced some part of the Polish society, which feared, in particular, that Czechoslovakia could fall under German influence. However, when analysing the Security Service documents, we can find quite numerous examples of various forms of protest and gestures of genuine, spontaneous solidarity with the southern neighbours. We should remember here that many people may have had a critical opinion about the invasion, but only part of them decided to protest openly. These were mainly "hostile utterances", as well as leaflets and "hostile inscriptions".

Some conclusions, unfortunately supported by a small base of evidence, can be drawn from 93 letters sent to the Polish Radio and Polish Television in the period of 21 August–17 September. According to the statistics drawn in the Letters Department of the Radio and Television Committee "Polish Radio and Television", 25 correspondents allegedly expressed their support for the invasion, and the remaining 68—their disapproval[213].

A frequent phenomenon comprised of so-called hostile utterances, which showed the aversion of the Poles to the actions of the Warsaw Pact's armed forces. The truth of official media reports was generally doubted. In

---

211 Mariusz Mazur, Nieoficjalne wzajemne stosunki Polaków, Czechów i Słowaków w okresie praskiej wiosny na łamach polskiej prasy, 196–198.
212 Ibid., 198–199.
213 Grzegorz Majchrzak, Poľské občianske protesty proti intervencii v Československu z pohľadu bezpečnostných dokumentov, 39.

turn, the SB noted a significant increase in interest in the broadcasts of "Radio Free Europe" and other Western radio stations broadcasting in Polish. The Polish Armed Forces participation in the invasion was perceived as a national disgrace and a violation of traditions of freedom. Terms such as: "invasion", "open aggression", "crime", "criminal incursion" were used. Sometimes, fears emerged that the intervention could trigger a new worldwide armed conflict, since the USA would not put up with the Warsaw Pact's armed forces staying in the territory of Czechoslovakia.[214] On August 22, Radio Free Europe reported: "In bars, restaurants and canteens, people voiced their dissatisfaction aloud. On the first day of the invasion, many PUWP activists reported "sick", fearing to show themselves to the people".[215]

By the end of August 1968, the SB noted 2,147 leaflets against the aggression on Czechoslovakia, with over half of them—1277—found in Warsaw[216]. Rather surprisingly, there were twice as many of them than in March '68. On the night of August 22, and the small hours of the next morning, in Brzeg (woj. Opole) the Communist era Police—Milicja Obywatelska (MO)—found nine leaflets with the slogans: "Gomułka, hands off Czechoslovakia" on the one side, and "For our freedom and yours" on the other side. On August 22 in the Central Department Store neighbourhood in Warsaw, leaflets were distributed, with the call: "Compatriots, defend the freedom of CSSR, compatriots, condemn aggression". Later new leaflets were thrown out of the CDS windows. Their authors had written: "Poles, condemn the aggression on the CSSR. The press is lying. Freedom for CSSR". On 24 August, from the same building, leaflets were again thrown down, with the content: "Shame on the aggressors shaming Poland and Socialism. Long live free CSSR!".[217]

---

214 Łukasz Kamiński, Ręce precz od Czechów! Polacy wobec inwazji na Czechosłowację w 1968 r. *Więź*, 2004, no 7, 80–81.
215 Rok 1968. Środek peerelu [1968. The middle of the Polish People's Republic], elaborated by A. Dębska, (Warszawa: Karta, 2008), 183.
216 Note by Henryk Piętek, Head of Department III of MSW on the comments concerning internal affairs in Czechoslovakia, 03.09.1968, In: Łukasz Kamiński, Grzegorz Majchrzak, eds., Operacja "Podhale". Służba Bezpieczeństwa wobec wydarzeń w Czechosłowacji 1968-1970 [Operation "Podhale". Security Service and the events in Czechoslovakia 1968-1970], (Warszawa: Instytut Pamięci Narodowej, 2008), 535.
217 Archive of the Institute of National Remembrance in Warsaw (AIPN), 0296/109, vol. 2, Kronika wydarzeń operacji "Podhale" (Chronicle of operation "Podhale"), (20 VIII - 8 IX 1968 r.), without pagination.

In Krakow, leaflets were found with the contents: "Long live Czechoslovakia" and "CSSR—we are with you". In Tarnow, leaflets, prepared by a group of activists from the Union of Socialist Youth, were thrown around: "We strongly protest against the assault on the kindred Czechoslovakia. Gomułka has shamed our nation in the world's eyes. In the name of the noblest possible cause, for our freedom and yours, we are with you, our Czech comrades. Long live free and independent Czechoslovakia." At the back, there was information about a protest meeting in Tarnow planned for 28 August, which, however, did not take place.[218]

The Poles distributed not only the leaflets they had prepared themselves, but also those smuggled from Czechoslovakia. It was just for this that, in the night of the 29/30th, two 18-year-olds—Władysław Juszczak and Roman Paluch—were detained in Głuchołazy. They had managed to give away just four leaflets, and the remaining ninety were taken away by the MO.[219] Several times, the leaflets appealed to participation in demonstrations against the invasion of Czechoslovakia. For example, on 22 and 23 August, in Warsaw, leaflets were distributed with information about a protest meeting in front of the Soviet Embassy on the following day.[220] Unfortunately, none of those demonstrations actually took place.

Next to the leaflets and "hostile inscriptions", posters appeared—but more rarely. The greatest number of them were found in Warsaw: just on August 23, they numbered over 40 in Hoża Street. Posters were also stuck up in the provinces. For example, on the morning of August 25, in Skierniewice, two posters were discovered, containing the slogans: "Fascists, get out of Prague!" and "End the Stalinist dictatorship", and in Szczecin two more: "1938—Hitler, 1968—Kosyghin" and "Bolsheviks, get out of the CSSR!"[221].

---

218 Julian Kwiek, Reakcje społeczeństwa województwa krakowskiego na wydarzenia w Czechosłowacji w 1968 roku w świetle dokumentów partyjnych [The reactions of the Krakow voivodeship society to the events in Czechoslovakia in 1968 in the light of party documents], In: Petr Blažek, Paweł Jaworski, Łukasz Kamiński, Rudolf Vévoda, eds., Między przymusową przyjaźnią a prawdziwą solidarnością. Czesi—Polacy—Słowacy 1938/39-1945-1989, Part II, (Warszawa: Instytut Pamięci Narodowej, 2009), 232.
219 AIPN, 0296/109, vol. 2, Chronicle of operation "Podhale".
220 AIPN, 0296/109, vol. 2, Chronicle of operation "Podhale".
221 Grzegorz Majchrzak, Poľské občianske protesty proti intervencii v Československu z pohľadu bezpečnostných dokumentov, 45.

Between the 21st and 31st of August, SB and MO noted 86 "hostile slogans" (the majority of them in Krakow—28).[222] As in the case of leaflets, there were twice as many of them than in March '68. Doubtless, one of the first places where they appeared was the road from Zakopane to the Morskie Oko mountain lake. As Maciej Włodek recalls, the slogans ("Anschluss shall not pass", "Down with the aggression", "Invaders, go home", "Hitler—Brezhnyev—Gomułka—Ulbricht—Kadar—Zhivkov") were made spontaneously by a group of people he was in when they had learned about the invasion of Czechoslovakia. Those slogans—as Włodek recalls—became a bombshell on the following day.[223] On the road from Bydgoszcz to Gdansk, in the neighbourhood of Augustowo, the slogans: "Long live free Czechoslovakia!" and "Long live Dubček!" appeared. They were equally frequently placed on the walls, e.g. in the night of 21/22 August, on the building of the Poviat Committee of the PUWP in Milanówek, near Warsaw: "Down with Soviet aggression in Czechoslovakia. Russians go home."[224] On the building of Cracow University of Technology, somebody wrote: "Death to the occupiers of CSSR".[225]

This phenomenon was so widespread that, on August 24, Deputy Minister Pietrzak warned, during a briefing with voivodship MO commanders: "A [phenomenon] both characteristic and unknown, until now, are slogans at the workplaces, in the streets and on the walls—made with oil paint or chalk. Until now, these kinds of inscriptions have been a rarity."[226] A number of satirical works, ridiculing the pro-intervention propaganda, became very popular. Many people, who later got involved in opposition activities, attached great importance to Jacek Tarkowski's song Hradec Kralove.[227]

---

222 Note by Henryk Piętek, Head of Department III of MSW on the comments concerning internal affairs in Czechoslovakia, 3 IX 1968, 535.
223 Maciej Włodek, Taternicy przeciw agresji na Czechosłowację ["Mountaineers" against aggression against Czechoslovakia], *Gazeta Wyborcza*, September 15, 2008.
224 Grzegorz Majchrzak, Poľské občianske protesty proti intervencii v Československu z pohľadu bezpečnostných dokumentov, 46.
225 Julian Kwiek, Reakcje społeczeństwa województwa krakowskiego na wydarzenia w Czechosłowacji w 1968 roku w świetle dokumentów partyjnych, 232.
226 Grzegorz Majchrzak, Poľské občianske protesty proti intervencii v Československu z pohľadu bezpečnostných dokumentov, 46.
227 Łukasz Kamiński, Ręce precz od Czechów! Polacy wobec inwazji na Czechosłowację w 1968 r., 84.

Symptoms of dissatisfaction also appeared at meetings of Party organizations on August 21. Members of the PUWP expressed their fears of possible armed conflict with the West. They also asked difficult questions, e.g. whether the army incursion was compliant with the statute of the Warsaw Pact; "if Czechoslovakia has her own army, what is the reason for assistance from the outside?" They asked for an explanation of the difference between the intervention of the USSR in Czechoslovakia and the involvement of the USA in Vietnam.

In the first days after the intervention, at least a few dozen people left the ranks of the PUWP in protest. The widest repercussions were triggered by the return of the party membership cards by employees of the Institute of History of the Polish Academy of Sciences: Dr. Bronisław Geremek, Dr. Krystyna Kersten and Prof. Tadeusz Łepkowski. The scale of this phenomenon is unknown, since no statistics were kept.[228]

More risky gestures of solidarity with the southern neighbours included laying flowers in front of the Czechoslovakian Embassy in Warsaw. On August 22, 1968, the "B" Bureau of SB, engaged in observation, noted three such cases. Persons detained for this reason, included Wojciech Łojkowski, a teacher from Pruszków, Danuta Danek, an employee of the Institute of Literary Research PAS and a 16-year-old student, Ryszard Kirszenbaum.[229]

A much safer and more frequent activity was the laying of flowers in front of the Czechoslovak Institute in Warsaw, which, unlike the country's embassy, was not so densely surrounded by the Police (MO). Here we should quote the description by Radio Free Europe of August 28:

> In front of the Centre of Czechoslovakian Culture building at 79 Marszałkowska Street, the Police were hurriedly removing bunches of flowers, laid there by the residents of Warsaw as a sign of solidarity with the kindred nations of Czechs and Slovaks [...] Hundreds of the capital's residents pass in silence along the Koszykowa Street next to the Czechoslovakian Embassy building. Stopping has been forbidden, the Embassy building is surrounded by Police guards [...] so they pass slowly, for nobody can forbid this yet. When passing the building [...] they bow their heads.[230]

---

228 Łukasz Kamiński, *Polská sjednocená dělnická strana a Pražske jaro*, 109–110.
229 AIPN, 0296/109, vol. 2, Chronicle of operation "Podhale".
230 Jan Ptaczek, Comment titled *"Warszawa wyraża sympatie dla Czechów i Słowaków. [Warsaw expresses sympathy for Czechs and Slovaks]*. Quoted following: Grzegorz Majchrzak, *Pol'ské občianske protesty proti intervencii v Československu z pohľadu bezpečnostných dokumentov*, 48.

Few people decided to publicly condemn Polish participation in the invasion of Czechoslovakia. In September 1968, Jerzy Andrzejewski wrote a letter to Edvard Goldstuecker, President of the Association of Czech Writers, expressing his "outrage, pain and shame" caused by the invasion of the Polish Armed Forces. For this, he was later harassed by the SB.[231]

Adam Giera was expelled from the Vocational School for Petty Officers in Brok, for he was deemed to be one of the leaders of the revolt against the intervention in Czechoslovakia.[232] In turn, Jerzy Gregorowicz, a student of Maria Curie-Skłodowska University in Lublin, was deprived of his scholarship for a critical remark on the participation of the Polish People's Armed Forces in the invasion on the southern neighbour, that he uttered during classes.[233]

It would seem that a safer form of protest was sending anonymous letters with protests. They were addressed to the embassies of Western countries (mainly of the United States) and of Czechoslovakia, as well as to the Polish authorities. Most likely, the majority of them never reached the addressees. This was the result of correspondence censorship (so-called "perlustration"), carried out in secrecy (except for the martial law period) in the period of the People's Republic of Poland, enhanced, of course, in a crisis situation. The censors stopped letters of a "leaflet character", or those containing expressions of support for the Czechs and Slovaks. And so, for example, on August 23, 1968, SB officers captured twelve postcards addressed to central institutions, and "containing primitive, vulgar text concerning the incursion of the Warsaw Pact's armed forces". In turn, on the 26th and 27th of August, a total of 54 letters to embassies were counted, including 27 letters to the Czechoslovak Embassy (one of them was recognized to have a "positive" character).[234]

Perlustration was applied to the whole correspondence with Czechoslovakia. SB was also interested in the correspondence with capitalist countries and in parts of domestic letters. Each day, a dozen or so thousand

---

231 Jerzy Eisler, *Polski rok 1968*, 749.
232 Przemysław Miśkiewicz, *Giera Adam*, In: Encyklopedia Solidarności. Opozycja w PRL 1976–1989 [Encyclopedia of Solidarity. Opposition in the People's Republic of Poland 1976–1989], vol. 1, (Warszawa: Volumen, 2010), 123.
233 Marcin Dąbrowski, *Gregorowicz Jerzy*. In: Encyklopedia Solidarności. Opozycja w PRL 1976–1989, vol. 2, (Warszawa: Volumen, 2012), 129.
234 AIPN, 0296/109, vol. 2, Chronicle of operation "Podhale".

letters were browsed, e.g. on August 22-23, almost 5500 in exchange with Czechoslovakia, 25,000 with capitalist countries and 21,000 domestic mailings.[235]

From time to time, more extreme forms of protest occurred. For example, in the night of August 22/23, 1968, a firecracker was thrown into the conference hall of the Poviat Committee of the PUWP in Kętrzyn. In turn, in Nowe Miasto, most probably in the night of 24/25 August, a monument to "Soviet and Polish heroic soldiers" was defiled by putting a tin garbage can on the head of a Red Army soldier. Two days later, in the cemetery of Soviet soldiers in Wrocław, swastikas were painted with oil paint on the posts of three entrance gates and on a tank standing on a plinth, while in Puławy, the monument to Ludwik Waryński, a Socialist movement activist, was daubed with red paint. However, the most daring and risky feat of this type was probably the tearing down (on August 21) of a board with Lenin's image from the highest peak of Polish Tatras—Rysy— by activists of the illegal "Ruch" organization: Stefan Niesiołowski and Wojciech Majda[236].

The Poles supported the Czechs and Slovaks also within Czechoslovakia. In Jičín, which, on September 7, became the scene of the most tragic incident connected with the participation of the Polish Armed Forces in the invasion, a drunken soldier, Stefan Dorna, shot two Czechs; two weeks earlier two Polish women employed in Czechoslovakia—Wiesława Moryń from Wołów and Helena Willas from Złotoryja—sat down in front of a microphone of one of the many illegal radio broadcasting stations. "In the name of a group of Polish workers present in the CSSR", they appealed to Polish soldiers to stop the armed intervention.[237]

On August 30, a Polish woman working in the Nova Paka locality, declared, in turn: "that we, employed Polish women, show solidarity with the Czechs and are against the incursion of the Polish army into the area of the CSSR". She also claimed that some Polish women, in order to show solidarity with their southern neighbours, "are wearing in their jacket lapels miniature CSSR flags" with the names of Svoboda, Dubček, Černik. Poles living in Czechoslovakia showed support for their southern

---

235 Grzegorz Majchrzak, Służba Bezpieczeństwa PRL a Praska Wiosna, 97.
236 Rok 1968. Środek peerelu, 185.
237 AIPN, 0296/109, vol. 2, Chronicle of operation "Podhale".

neighbours in other ways too. A campaign of collecting signatures under a petition to the authorities of the People's Republic of Poland, for the withdrawal of Polish soldiers from the CSSR, was organized in Olbrachcice, near Czech Cieszyn.[238]

The invasion of Czechoslovakia was also protested against by the Polish diaspora, mainly in the West. It was condemned by the authorities of the Republic of Poland in exile and by all the major opposition milieus. A special statement was issued by the Polish Writers' Association in Exile. In the statement, the Association declared that, in view of the fact that writers in Poland are forced to be silent with Communist terror and cannot openly express their views [...] protests against the illegal and brutal conquest of Czechoslovakia by Soviet Russia and, at the same time, condemns the government of People's Poland, which, against the will and traditions of the Polish nation, obeying their Soviet command-givers, included the Polish Army in the occupation, insulting, in this way, the name of our soldiers.[239]

Of course, the protests were not limited to declarations or statements. And so, for example, on August 23, a few thousand Poles demonstrated in front of the PRP Embassy in London. Their demonstration was preceded by a meeting in Hyde Park, with speeches by the leaders of the Polish diaspora (among others, a former Ambassador of RP in Great Britain, Edward Raczyński). A resolution was adopted, which expressed solidarity with Czechoslovakia, condemned the invasion of that country and demanded immediate the withdrawal of Polish armed forces from the CSSR.[240] From time to time, there were also individual initiatives. The best-known case was that of Sławomir Mrożek, who, in a letter published in French press, condemned the incursion of the Warsaw Pact's armed forces into Czechoslovakia.[241]

The most dramatic form of protest was chosen by Ryszard Siwiec, a sixty-year-old accountant from Przemyśl. He decided to shock his compatriots and wake up their consciences by sacrificing his own life. He planned his protest carefully. He acquired a pass to the central harvest

---

238 Grzegorz Majchrzak, Poľské občianske protesty proti intervencii v Československu z pohľadu bezpečnostných dokumentov, 51.
239 Ibid., 52.
240 Ibid., 53.
241 Jerzy Eisler, *Polski rok 1968*, 749.

celebrations in Warsaw, wrote down his last will, bought a solvent, prepared a white and red flag with the inscription "For your freedom and ours", and finally recorded on an audio tape his political manifesto, in which he criticised Soviet imperialism and the oppression of smaller nations.[242]

On September 8, 1968, during the central harvest celebrations at the Warsaw 10th Anniversary Stadium, in the presence of a 100,000 people and the state authorities, Ryszard Siwiec poured the solvent over his body and set it on fire. He died four days later in hospital. On him, leaflets were found, beginning with the words: "I protest against the unprovoked aggression on brotherly Czechoslovakia". Though his deed was witnessed by thousands of people, Siwiec failed to achieve his goal. People did not understand what this was about. The Security Service informed those standing closest to Siwiec, that this was an accidental ignition of a drunkard. It was only in Spring 1969, already after the self-immolation of Jan Palach, that the news of Siwiec's deed was broadcast by Radio Free Europe.[243]

Polish expressions of solidarity with the Czechs and Slovaks did not end in August or September 1968. In October—when students returned to universities—an unexpected popularity was enjoyed by the Czech language course. In November, leaflets found near student dorms in Krakow, expressed sympathy for Dubček's party, and contained the slogans: "Shame on the invaders", "Withdraw the army from CSSR" and "We condemn aggression on Czechoslovakia".[244] In turn, on January 25, 1969, in Wroclaw, leaflets—with obituaries stuck on—were signed by "Wroclaw students" and alluded to the self-immolation of the Czech student Jan Palach in mid-January, 1969.[245]

Because of the protests against the invasion, and for solidarity shown to the Czechs and Slovaks, over a hundred people were detained, and a

---

242 Łukasz Kamiński, Ręce precz od Czechów! Polacy wobec inwazji na Czechosłowację w 1968 r., 87.

243 Ibid., 87–88. More on that subject, see Petr Blažek, *Ryszard Siwiec 1909–1968*, (Praha: Ústav pro studium totalitních režimů, 2010); Jan Draus, Maciej Szymanowski, eds., *Living torches. Testimonies of protest and solidarity in the face of the invasion of Czechoslovakia in 1968*, (Warszawa: Wydawnictwo Sejmowe, 2018), 33–55.

244 Julian Kwiek, Reakcje społeczeństwa województwa krakowskiego na wydarzenia w Czechosłowacji w 1968 roku w świetle dokumentów partyjnych, 234.

245 Łukasz Kamiński, Reakcje społeczeństwa Dolnego Śląska na interwencję wojsk Układu Warszawskiego, 216.

further few hundred were called for "prophylactic and warning conversations"; a few dozen appeared in front of administrative and penal boards, and a more than a dozen were sentenced to up to three years in prison. The sentences might not seem very impressive, but things start looking different when we recall the case of the 20-year old, Joanna Helander, a student of Romance studies at Jagiellonian University. In late Autumn 1968, together with her sister and another colleague she hung a poster with the slogan, "Muscovites! Hands off Czechoslovakia", out of her student dorm window. This 10-minute protest ended with her 10-month imprisonment. Moreover, after leaving prison, her student rights were suspended, and she decided to emigrate.[246]

The charge against Teresa Stodolniak was that "in the period from 21 August 1968 through 16 October 1968, she prepared and distributed in Warsaw, leaflets, posters and slogans, which contained false information on the events in Czechoslovakia, capable of causing public unrest". Despite having two young children, she was sentenced to a year in prison by the court. At the turn of October and November 1968, the SB broke down a group of at least 30 people, who had been producing and distributing leaflets starting from March. After August 21, the group distributed a few types of leaflets in relatively large quantities (a few hundred each). 14 people were arrested, of which seven were sentenced to a year or a year-and-a-half in prison.[247]

Summing up the attitude of Communist authorities of the PRP, we should say that Władysław Gomułka, for reasons evident to him, supported the aggression on Czechoslovakia, and then the policy of normalization. He had a critical attitude not only towards Dubček, but also to his successor, Gustav Husák. Gomułka accused him of too slow progress of the normalization and pointed out mistakes. Hence, the relations between the PUWP and the CPCz remained rather cold for a long time. The situation changed only after the power in Poland was taken by Edward Gierek,

---

246 Agnieszka Pustułka, Każda z 10 minut trwania protestu kosztowała ją miesiąc *więzienia* [Each of the 10 minutes of the protest cost her a month in prison], *Polski Dziennik Zachodni,* August 23, 2013.
247 Łukasz Kamiński, Ręce precz od Czechów! Polacy wobec inwazji na Czechosłowację w 1968 r., 90–91.

a pragmatic Communist from Silesia, who strove to develop economic cooperation with Czechoslovakia.[248]

Due to the absence of public opinion surveys, we cannot precisely determine the distribution of individual attitudes in Polish society. In the first days after the launching of the invasion of Czechoslovakia, condemnation of the aggression and outrage towards it dominated decisively. With time, as a result of propaganda, the circle of people accepting the intervention gradually grew. All gestures of protest and solidarity with the Czechs and Slovaks should be appreciated. They required overcoming not only the prejudices accrued over decades, but also the fear—which was fully justified—of possible repressions. The gestures mentioned above were not made any easier either by the brutal quashing of the March '68 protests by the authorities or by the holiday period. Yet, in August 1968, and in the subsequent months, a forced, propaganda-based friendship became momentarily replaced by true solidarity.

---

248 More on that subject, see Mirosław Szumiło, Vedení Polské lidové republiky vůči normalizaci v Československu (1969–1971) [Leadership of the Polish People's Republic against Normalization in Czechoslovakia (1969–1971)], In: Jiří Petraš, Libor Svoboda, eds., *Jaro '68 a nástup normalizace. Československo v letech 1968–1971* [Spring '68 and the beginning of normalization. Czechoslovakia in the years 1968–1971], (České Budějovice-Praha: Ústav pro studium totalitních režimů, 2017), 271–281.

08
The Bulgarians and the Prague Spring, 1968

Mihail Gruev
Institute for Studies of the Recent Past, Sofia

Usually the outlook for Bulgaria in the years of the communist regime is summarized by the metaphor: the "quietest shack in the socialist camp". Indeed, it seems to be true, but only from the Western and Central European point of view. If we change the perspective and look at Bulgaria from the inside out, or in the context of the other Balkan autocratic regimes, we will see a much more colourful and complex picture in which the echo of the Prague Spring is central. Moreover, this phenomenon for the entire Eastern Bloc and its accompanying events so shocked and transformed the Bulgarian intelligentsia and the whole society that they were no longer the same. How did this come to be, and what are the boundaries and manifestations of this transformation? In order to answer these questions, it is necessary first to outline the starting positions of the main social actors in the country at the beginning of the Prague Spring and, above all, to review the state of the Bulgarian Communist Party in 1968.

At that time, it was governed solely by Todor Zhivkov, reasonably regarded as one of Moscow's closest Communist leaders in Eastern Europe. His nomination for party boss in 1954, and then prime minister in 1962, was entirely due to Khrushchev. Removing the old guard of Dimitrov-Chervenkov one by one from the narrow party leadership since 1956, he simultaneously strengthened his own position and eliminated real and potential competitors in power. This, however, does not made him an anti-Stalinist, but a mere conjuncture functionary, who saw in change of wind coming from Moscow after the XX Congress of the CPSU, a golden chance for his own endorsement. However, after the April 1956 Plenary Session of the Central Comity of the BCP, where Zhivkov got rid of Chervenkov's tutelage, his rhetoric sounded relatively reformist and liberal. This was short-lived—contining only until the Hungarian uprising of the Autumn of the same year, when both he himself and the group around him became painfully aware that any further move towards liberalization could irritate the system. Then a reverse process of stagnation and creeping re-Stalinization followed, but without repression and various forms of violence reaching the scale and totality established in the first years after the Communist Party came into power. To preserve Khrushchev's confidence in him, which he clearly identified as a crucial condition for his stay at the top, Zhivkov took a series of steps towards isolation from the senior party leadership—simultaneously from both the Stalinists and the possible revisionists. His manoeuvres in this period can be compared to driving a car in the middle of a narrow road so it cannot be overtaken from either the left or the right. The withdrawal of Khrushchev from power in 1964 raised the hopes of party veterans long out of power that the new strong man in the Kremlin, Leonid Brezhnev, would replace Zhivkov with his own minion. Similarly, such expectations with regard to their own leaders exist in other Eastern European Communist parties. Brezhnev, however, was not in a hurry with the castlings. It took some time for him to find out whether, in Bulgaria and in the other countries, it was a matter of personal loyalty to Khrushchev, or loyalty in principle to the Kremlin, regardless of who was in charge. Zhivkov assessed the importance of the moment and did his best to prove to Brezhnev that the latter was true. He quickly condemned Khrushchev's "volunteerism" and ranks among the first to have praised the new Soviet leader.

However, the Kremlin's upheaval has intensified various atomized Stalinist and Maoist groups in the BCP, including its broad leadership, the Central Committee. In 1965, the largest attempt at a coup against Zhivkov was exposed—from the so-called Gorunya group, including members and candidate members of the CC and army and militia generals. The group viewed Zhivkov as a traitor of the authentic Communist idea and admired simultaneously Stalin and Mao.[249] Although its head was forced to commit suicide, and another 12 of its members were severely convicted, smaller and weaker Neo-Stalinist and Maoist groups were revealed by the State Security authorities in various locations throughout the country in the years to come.[250] At the party congress of 1966, under the pressure of the Kremlin, Zhivkov was forced, despite his personal dislike of them, to return to

---

249 Ivan Bakalov, *Furst-Person Putsch Makers. The Plots Against Todor Zhivkov* (Sofia: Millenium, 2008) 15–76.
250 Mihail Doktorov, *In a Fight with the Octopus. The "Second Center" in the Struggle against Zhivkovists 1965–1968* (Sofia: Kota, 1993).

the Politburo members figures of the old Dimitrov-Chervenkov's guards. All this deprived Zhivkov of opportunities for more serious political maneuvers, and he himself had no desire for something like that. On the contrary, he strove to win Brezhnev's trust with all his might, showering him constantly with praise, state awards and expensive gifts. The latter began to reach out to members of his family with whom he also tried to establish informal ties. By 1968, Zhivkov had earned Brezhnev's trust and acquired the reputation of one of his most trusted puppets among East European Communist leaders. Nevertheless, until the beginning of the Prague Spring, he was trying to carry out some reforms in the economic sphere aimed at bringing some of the enterprises in the country closer to the market principles, in linking production to demand and wages, with the profits of the economic subjects themselves. Perhaps this is the reason for the noticeable delay in his negative assessment of what was happening in Czechoslovakia after the January plenum of the CCP's CC and the arrival of Dubcek in power. At first, he was apprehending the overthrow of Novotný with concern, not only for his excellent contacts with him, but also because of the uncertainty whether Brezhnev had not finally stepped into a staged replacement of Khrushchev's Eastern European political party functionaries. Very soon, however, it became obvious that Dubcek was not Brezhnev's man, and that Zhivkov was the one who took firmly and categorically the position of one of the hardliners in the Political Consultative Committee of the Warsaw Pact.

    The first public speeches of the Bulgarian Communist leader against the Prague Spring were at the Warsaw Pact summit in Sofia on March 6 and 7, 1968. Before the meeting, he held a personal meeting with Brezhnev and Kosygin, who informed him of the Soviet position on the issue. From that moment on, it became his position. As a host, it gained more weight. The resolution of the meeting still expresses formal support for the new Czechoslovak leadership, but it is explicitly underlined that the leadership should start a determined struggle with the anti-Socialist forces in the country.[251] Two weeks later, at a meeting in Dresden on March 23 and 24, the criticism expressed in Sofia turned into a massive attack. Although formally the meeting was declared unofficial and only in countries neighbouring the Czechoslovakia, a Bulgarian delegation led by the second person in the Bulgarian Communist Party at that time Stanko Todorov

---

251 Central State Archive (CSA), domain 1B, list 58, archive unit 1, sheet 90–101.

appeared there. Zhivkov was visiting Turkey at that time. This manoeuvre was used to avoid inviting Ceausescu, who initially disapproved of interference in the interior affairs of any East European country. It is known that for security reasons, it was decided not to keep minutes for the meeting, and its participants not to make written comments.[252] Todorov's cautious position at this meeting and Zhivkov's absence from it made some observers to see in this some purposeful strategy of restraint and moderation on the Bulgarian side. In fact, no such thing can be said, since Todorov was probably afraid of being suspected by Zhivkov in his plan to overwhelm him with servility, and he spoke Russian very poorly. In fact, at this meeting, the anti-Czechoslovak coalition of the five countries was formed, which began to act in concert, under the dictatorship of Moscow, for the crushing of the Prague Spring. In his report on the meeting, which he said will live on in memory, during the Plenary Session of the CC of the Bulgarian Communist Party on March 29, 1968, Todorov repeats Zhivkov's old thesis that, in principle, reforms to the Communist parties are necessary, giving the exemple of the BCP, which itself had been rebuilt in 1956. He said, unlike the other Communist leaders, he does not think the situation is out of control, and he is still talking about the need for a "serious ideological struggle" rather than a physical one.[253]

A month later, on April 23, Zhivkov arrived in Prague at the head of a party-state delegation to sign a new treaty of friendship, cooperation and mutual assistance for a period of 20 years. His mission was more of an intelligence nature. From the minutes of the meeting between the two leaderships, it becomes clear that although mutual exchanges of kindness are possible, a common language between them is impossible:

> "Dubcek: This year for the first time a secret ballot was held in the party, we had censorship.
> Zhivkov: There is no censorship in our country, but we have strict control and we are holding fast."[254]

There was a new general meeting of the already formed five in Moscow in May, during which Zhivkov had already furiously attacked the Prague Spring and emerged as one of its most irreconcilable opponents, along

---

252 CSA, domain 1B, list 58, archive unit 3, sheet 2–3.
253 Ibid., sheet 39–40.
254 CSA, domain 1B, list 60, archive unit 7, sheet 28.

with Walter Ulbricht and Władysław Gomulka. Most likely, the decision to enter with troops in Czechoslovakia was taken here, still as a backup option, if the others do not work. Some suggest Zhivkov was the one who officially put the military operation on the table. Incidentally, this was the version that the Bulgarian foreign minister, Petar Mladenov, propounded five years later at one of the party plenums, probably led by his desire to yet again flatter his boss.[255] This seems exaggerated, as it is clear that it was Brezhnev's decision, and the others just succumbed. On the other hand, both Polish and East German leadership offer the same. It is a fact, however, that Zhivkov sought to be perceived as a spokesman for Brezhnev. It is said that joking with himself, he described the dependencies in Bulgaria in the following way: "Where it is not convenient to go comrade Brezhnev, usually I go, and where it is not convenient that I go, comrade Peter Tanchev (the leader of the Communists' allied Agrarian party in the country) goes, and where it is not convenient him to go, too, then the patriarch goes".

In his speeches, both in Moscow and Warsaw on July 14 and 15, Zhivkov clearly states that his fears are not only for Czechoslovakia but also for the whole socialist system. Such thoughts also excite the other authors of the Warsaw ultimate letter to the Czechoslovak leadership.[256] That's why they all start discussing the intervention no longer as a backup but as a major option to get out of the situation.

The Bulgarian Communist leader has every reason to worry about the real possibility of major upheaval in society, and about the sympathy that increasingly widespread circles of the intelligentsia and youth were beginning to manifest and express publically towards the Prague Spring. This is the place to note that since late 19th century the Czechoslovak community in Bulgaria, end especially the Czechs, enjoyed the outstanding sympathy of local society. In a broad range of public spheres, branches of science, in the arts, as well as in the overall modernization of Bulgarian society during the decades after the 1878 Liberation from the Ottomans, the Czechs played a widely recognized leadership role. This was the reason why their sizeable diaspora in Sofia, and in some other big cities of the

---

255 CSA, domain 1B, list 58, archive unit 84, sheet 128. Quoted by: Kalinova, Evgenia, Baeva, Iskra. *Bulgarian Transitions 1939-2010*, Sofia, Padigma, 2010, 178.

256 See more detail in: Nikolov, Aleksandar. "Fraternal Assistance and Bulgaria", in *The Hot Summer of '68. The Prague Spring* (Sofia: Dr Zhelyu Zhelev Foundation, 2013), 20–40.

country as well, enjoyed unquestioned authority and prestige. The sympathies went both ways as the Czechs in turn saw Bulgarians as a close Slavic nation that had been revived to an independent statehood after several centuries of foreign rule. What they were doing in Bulgaria was a projection of their own aspirations for independence, national recognition and excellence. The social capital, which the Czechoslovak community commanded in Bulgaria, undoubtedly amplified the influences coming from Prague in 1968. This was yet another reason why the Communist leadership in Sofia was more anxious by the repercussions that the Czechoslovak developments had domestically compared to all other intra-bloc crises before and after. Of course, the fact that the Czechs and Slovaks had the highest share of foreign tourists who frequented the Black Sea coast—at least because they didn't have much choice in term of destinations—should not be ignored. Some of them had been visiting Bulgaria every year, thus having established their own contacts in the country and being able to wield a stronger influence on various groups of society.[257]

At the same time as running all these diplomatic shuttles, Sofia was actively preparing for the 9th World Youth and Students Festival. In the context of what was happening in Czechoslovakia, this casual event, funded primarily by the Soviet Union and other Eastern European countries through the so-called World Federation of Democratic Youth as a form of maintaining a loose ideological network between leftist and pro-communist youth and student organizations around the world, acquired unexpected dimensions.[258] Still, however, the hosts in Sofia were not at a clear about this to Central Committee of Komsomol, so the event was popularized loudly as another ideological and propaganda event. Thus, by Todor Zhivkov releasing pigeons at Sofia's Vasil Levski Stadium on July 28, 1968, the festival started. Yet in the middle of July, the festival delegations had begun to arrive in the country. The total number of participants reached 20,000 people. Never before had the country been visited by so many young people from all over the world. Indeed, at least half of them were from Eastern European countries, well-disciplined and instructed

---

257 See more detail in: Ivanova, Maya. *Tourism under Supervision. Balkantourist—the Beginning of the International and Mass Tourism in Bulgaria* (Sofia: Ciela, 2018) 213–290.
258 The original idea was to constitute something like a youth international of Communists and left-leaning Socialist organizations, holding its festivals every five years in the capitals of pro-Soviet or non-aligned countries. The first one was held in 1947 in Prague.

Komsomolts (with the exception of the Czechoslovak delegation). Many of the youth organizations of the Western European Communists also sent their ideologically straightforward representatives. Nevertheless, there were 7000 to 8000 "unstable, prone to bourgeois fashion and morals" young, a demographic that is hard to control. Among them were hipsters and hippies, anarchists, drug addicts, wandering fans of nudism and free love, and so on. In short, exporters of "ideological subversion" among Bulgarian youth, to be countered.[259] The regime and State Security in particular took a number of preventive measures. First of all, the Bulgarian delegation led by the secretary of the Komsomol Central Committee, Petar Mladenov (the man who in 1989 will replace Zhivkov briefly) was selected by extremely loyal and straightforward Komsomolts. The summer holidays of all employees in the State Security system were suspended. Additional 500 Komsomolts were being mobilized in kind of voluntary units to counter possible provocations by Czechoslovak agents or other "unhealthy forces", entering into verbal debates and, where necessary, in physical struggles with the enemy. From Sofia and the Black Sea resorts, which also featured festival events, about 6,000 thieves, beggars, prostitutes, mentally ill and "enemy elements" were displaced. Special efforts were made to expand the agency with taxi drivers, translators, hotel staff, and all those who were about to have direct contact with the participants in the festival. A further 450 officers and sergeants from the State Security Committee reserves were also summoned and made available to the National Preparatory Committee of the festival.[260] Separately from this, "guests with obscene appearance" were stopped and returned yet at the borders. This included those with long-hair, beards, even too narrow or scuffed trousers—anyone who bore the external signs of a subculture. The Bulgarian authorities are especially vigilant with regard to arrivals from Czechoslovakia. Their number is enormous—500 are the official members of the delegation, a part from 380 arriving as tourists and 80 journalists. Already at the border check point Kalotina, 25 Czech and Slovak hipsters were brought back because of their 'obscene' appearance.[261] Nevertheless, the State Security recognized the great conceptual motivation of the entire delegation, its

---

259 See more detail in: Gruev, Mikhail. *Youth Subcultures in Bulgaria in the 1970s and the 1980s: Critique and Humanism*, 1–2, 2014, 49–72.
260 Dossier Commission, domain 1, list 10, archive unit 445, sheet 116.
261 Ibid., archive unit 697, sheet 133.

desire to popularize the ideas of the Prague Spring in front of the Bulgarian society, and the festival as a whole, to openly demonstrate "socialism with a human face", as the Czechs and Slovaks understood it.[262] The authorities did not miss the deep sympathy with which the citizens of Sofia and especially the young people viewed the public manifestations of the representatives of Prague and Bratislava. It can be said that the festival was planned as a profoundly casual event aimed at popularizing the regime outside, but it had the opposite effect—it opened the eyes of thousands of Bulgarians and led to their apparent distancing from the regime. These tendencies were particularly clearly manifested in the weeks following the aggression.

On August 20 and 21, the Soviet-led troops of the five launched the Operation "Danube"—the occupation of the whole of Czechoslovakia. Two Bulgarian motor racing regiments (12th and 22nd) with a total number of about 2200 people, based on the Turkish border, participated in their composition. It was an isolated area in which other information than the official one did not penetrate. Already in July, their squad was transferred to training in the Soviet Union. This is the reason why, until the entry of these parts into the country, they were absolutely convinced that they had to free the people, who were waiting for them, from the "imperialist clique of Dubcek" trying to manipulate the people. That's why the frontal collision of these very young people with the reality in the country led to such severe psychological consequences. Their occupying area was central Slovakia and included the areas of Banska Bistrica, Zvolen and Brezno, as well as the Ruzyne Airport (along with the Soviet troops).

> This is how the great Bulgarian writer Georgi Markov describes the reaction among the intelligentsia in Sofia in his essay *When the Clocks Stop*: "In Sofia people were surprised and shocked. In the first hours, it seemed to all of us that there was some misunderstanding. The newspapers were late, because, as it was later understood, they had to change the printed message of the invasion. In the first version, it was reported that troops came at the invitation of the new government of the Czechoslovak People's Republic, and then changed in the sense that the entry was at the invitation of the workers and party groups. [...]
> Later that day, phones rang into the homes of the more prominent citizens; journalists, reporters—either from the radio or from the newspapers—rang to find the inevitable 'speeches' that would support the military action. To honour the Bulgarian intelligentsia it can be said that no reputable name has been found to have responded positively to the Bulgarian intervention in Czechoslovakia."[263]

---

262 Ibid., domain 24, list 1, archive unit 34, sheet 77–78.
263 Markov, Georgi. *New in Abstentia Reports for Bulgaria* (Sofia: Bulgarski pisatel, 1991), 167.

Despite the obvious sympathy of the Bulgarian intelligentsia to the Prague Spring and compassion to the Czechs and Slovaks, there are very few who decided to protest. Among them, a group of university students—historians from the Sofia University, who distributed about 200 posters with the content: "Get out the troops of Zhivkov, the Marionette, of the Czechoslovak Republic", was important. When the group, led by Edward Genov, learned about the protest organized by several Soviet citizens on the Red Square, they prepared 217 leaflets with the text: "Five Soviet Communists made a demonstration on Red Square. What are you doing?", as well as: "Five Soviet citizens have expressed solidarity with the Czechoslovak Republic, have received severe sentences. People, watch!" Leaflets were spread in Sofia and Plovdiv. In the beginning of 1969 the group was unveiled and three of the participants received sentences with different terms of imprisonment.[264] State security also revealed other small groups, writing leaflets or just graffiti against the invasion in Czechoslovakia. Among them, the Ruse group was particularly daring, and the famous writer Germinal Chivikov was also involved. Three of the participants also received effective sentences.

The most significant resonance of the Prague Spring in Bulgaria, however, was expressed not so much in the bold but still isolated actions of these small groups of valiant young people, but in the great breakthrough among the silent majority of Bulgarian society. The other key consequence of what happened was the gradual and almost invisible but irreversible process of erosion of the tacit consensus reached at that time about the legitimacy of the regime itself. Thirdly, this is the start and slow breakdown between the intelligentsia and the party bureaucracy. I will quote again the writer Georgi Markov, who exquisitely summarized all of this:

> "In its half-century existence, the Soviet system experienced not one or two convulsions, but on August 21, 1968, something irreparably scary happened—ideology denied the ideals in whose name it existed, or as, the night of the same day, one Bulgarian communist said desperately: "Today they buried the October Revolution." For all those who had taken the Aurora's gunshot as the birth moment of ideals, hopes, illusions, dreams of some vaguely beautiful, new human life, for those who fanatically preserved this feeling throughout so many painful years, the date of August 21 was the end."[265]

---

264 http://oshte-info.de-zorata.de/oshte.info/004/00104/08/2308/01.htm
265 Markov, Georgi. p. 165.

09
Operation "Danube"

Michal Štefanský
Institute of History, Slovak Academy of Sciences, Bratislava

The operation 'Danube' was the cover name of the invasion of the armies of the Warsaw Pact: Soviet Union, Poland, Hungary and Bulgaria. The military operation started on the 20th of August 1968 at 2300 hours, Central European time, when the armies of the above-mentioned states responded to the signal Vltava—666 and set off from their concentration centres. The army commanders, divisions, regiments and battalions opened one of the three envelopes assigned to them for operation 'Danube'. Three envelopes containg three alternatives: *'Danube'*, *'Danube—Channel'* and *'Danube— Channel—Globe'*. Except for the plan 'Danube', the other envelopes were destroyed in front of Chiefs of Staff.[266] Before that came the order to mark the military technologies of the invasion armies with white stripes. Military technologies without these (Czechoslovak) were to be neutralized during the operation, shooting was allowed only on order of higher commanders of the invasion armies. Even nowadays, the operation plans 'Danube— Channel' and 'Danube—Channel—Globe' are shrouded in mystery and about this, we can only express the opinion that they could have contained plans to advance further to the West, or to the Balkans, occupying Yugoslavia and Romania. It must be declared that this opinion is not based on accessible documents.

By August 25, 1968, there were 27 invasion divisions in full combat status in Czechoslovakia, out of these, 12 were tank divisions, 13 motor rifle divisions, airborne division and air army with all its resources, missiles included. Heavy fighting technologies were represented by 6 300 tanks, 2 000 cannons, 550 combat and 250 transport aircrafts[267]. Czechoslovak army consisted in the year 1968 of 10 divisions, that is 200 000 soldiers

---

[266] http://militera.lib.ru./h20c2/08html.Istoria vojn:Rossia (ZSSR) v vojnach vtoroj poloviny XX.veka. Čechoslovakia.
[267] *Operace "Dunaj": vojáci a Pražské jaro 1968: studie a dokumenty.* Praha: ÚSD AV ČR, 1994, p. 118–119.

concentrated on the western border of the country. Combat readiness was ordered in six out of 20 military districts in the Soviet Union with 85–100 divisions and further 70–80 divisions were in combat readiness in the states of Warsaw Pact. Soviet strategy units with nuclear armament were brought to combat readiness too. The disproportionate superiority of the Warsaw Pact armies served probably to cause fear and perhaps even to enlarge the invasion further to the West.

In spite of the preparation of five divisions, the army of East Germany did not participate in the invasion. On Soviet orders, two German divisions stopped on the border with Czechoslovakia and remained in readiness for combat until the end of October 1968. Only smaller German linking and reconnaissance units entered the territory of Czechoslovakia as part of the Soviet army.[268]

The military invasion within the operation 'Danube' followed basically two large aims: to stop the reform process in Czechoslovakia, reasoning that it posed the threats of a counterrevolutionary coup and of Czechoslovakia leaving the Soviet bloc. The second aim was a permanent deployment of Soviet armies in Czechoslovakia, an important geopolitical and military-strategic space close to NATO. The Czechoslovak-Soviet agreement from 1965 on the construction of three nuclear storage facilities in the territory of the Czech Republic was an important step towards positioning the Soviet armies in Czechoslovakia, these facilities were not finished yet in 1968. Secret debates during the year 1967 and the first half of 1968 on positioning of the Soviet armies in the territory of Czechoslovakia were not successful. In order to reach the aims of the Soviet leadership, Soviet generals spreaded during the year 1968 false information that the border with Germany was not secured enough and the Czechoslovak army was in decay.

Already before the 21st of August 1968, there had been three attempts to perform the 'entry' of Soviet armies in Czechoslovakia. The first attempt consisted in the plan of General Jashkin's division to pass the Polish-Czechoslovak border around Těšín and occupy the headquarters of the Central and Western military sphere of the Czechoslovak army in Tábor

---

[268] Rudiger Wencke, "Nacionaľnaja narodnaja armia GDR v Prage nezadejstvovalai," in *"Pražskaja vesna" i meždunarodnyj krizis 1968 goda* (Moskva: Demokratia, 2010), 393–404.

and in Příbrami. From the east, one division of the 38th Soviet army was to occupy the headquarters of the East military sphere of the Czechoslovak army in Trenčín. The occupation of the military headquarters would paralyze the Czechoslovak army. This attempt in May 1968 was not successful. The second attempt was connected with the training exercise 'Šumava' in the Czechoslovak territory, apart from the Soviet army units, also Polish, Hungarian and German units participated. The facts about the 'Šumava' training reveal it was in preparation to occupy the Czechoslovak territory. It did not have a particular excuse, so this plan was never executed. The third attempt from the end of July 1968 did not happen because in Čierna nad Tisou in the Czechoslovak territory, there were Soviet-Czechoslovak debates of the highest party and governmental representatives on the solution of the Czechoslovak crisis. By the end of July 1968, the military plans for invasion were in fact finished together with the preparation of documents (statements to the Czechoslovak army, to the Czechoslovak people and others)[269].

The preparation of the Warsaw Pact troops' invasion had begun already in the spring of 1968. Soviet leadership and its allies applied political, ideological and military pressure to Czechoslovakia to stop the process of reformation. The criticism of the reforms served to show the threat of Czechoslovakia leaving the Soviet bloc, which would threaten not only the countries of the Warsaw Pact but also the peace and security in Europe. Military manoeuvres in the neighbouring countries but, in particular, the military training 'Šumava' in the territory of Czechoslovakia were already fulfilling the tasks of military preparations for the invasion.

Soviet preparations for the intervention had begun as early as February 1968, with agitation by students who spoke Czech at the University of Saint Petersburg in the Soviet Union. In April 1968, the Commander of airborne division, V. F. Margelov received the order to prepare the division for landing in the territory of Czechoslovakia and for controlling the Czechoslovak army. Military preparations for the invasion in April 1968 are confirmed by other sources. General Alexander Majorov, Commander of the 38th Soviet army, states in his memoirs that on the 12th of April he was shown a map at the headquarters in Lviv—an order for the 38th army

---

4. Daniel Povolný, *Operace Dunaj. Krvavá odpoveď Varšavské smlouvy na pražské jaro 1968* (Praha: Akademia, 2018), 52–65, 66–130, 151–181.

for "the invasion to Czechoslovakia with the aim to suppress and destroy Czechoslovak counterrevolution".[270] General Majorov arrived in Trenčín on August 22, 1968 and set his crew up at the headquarters of the Eastern military sphere. Later Majorov was head of a group of Soviet armies temporarily placed at the headquarters in Milovice.

The schedule for beginning the operation 'Danube' was coordinated with the conservative group in the Presidency of the Central Committee KSČ. Alois Indra, Vasil Biľak, Drahomír Kolder, Bedřich Švestka, Antonín Kapek were in this group, the later four had signed the so called 'letter of invitation' asking the Soviet party for help, military one included. The co-ordination of the procedure of Indra's group was debated with Brezhnev on the 18th of August, when the Soviet Politburo approved the date of the invasion. Indra informed Brezhnev that his group would cause a split on the meeting of the Presidency on the 20th of August 1968 and would make a coup and take over the power from Dubček and his supporters. Subsequently, the government and the parliament would approve changes and talk to the citizens. Indra promised Brezhnev that the letter of invitation would be signed within 20–21 August also by other 50 representatives of KSČ and of the state and the signatures would serve as a reason for the entry of the armies. However, the development went in a different direction to the one planned by the conservative group. It was not possible to make a coup because the Presidency of the Central Committee approved a statement saying the armies entered without an invitation of party and government representatives of Czechoslovakia and was a breach of relations between the socialist countries and of international law. The conservative group failed to form a collaborative government and a large wave of resistance rose against the occupant. A spontaneous resistance manifested itself in three ways: by refusing the cooperation with the occupying armies, by claiming loyalty towards Czechoslovak legal representatives (Dubček, Svoboda, Černík) and by criticizing the collaborationists (Biľak, Viliam Šalgovič, Indra and others), as well as by paralysation of the information transmitted by Soviet propaganda and its substitution by information on the radio, television, newspapers, leaflets, texts on buildings and others. The citizens' resistance impeded the forming of a collaborative

---

270 Alexandr Majorov, *Vtorženie Čechoslovakia* (Moskva: Izdateľstvo "Prava čeloveka", 1998), 23.

government. In spite of huge military superiority, the political power remained in the hands of Czechoslovak legal representatives and the Soviet leadership with Brezhnev had to search for a solution in negotiation with Dubček, after his release from internment. Intenred alongside Dubček on the 21st of August were also O. Černík—Prime Minister, Jozef Smrkovský—Head of Parliament, František Krieger—Head of National Front, Bohumil Šimon and Jozef Špaček—members of Presidency of the Central Committee KSČ.

The invasion armies entered Czechoslovakia from everywhere. From the north, the divisions of the Northern group of Soviet troops in Poland came, as well as the 38th Soviet troop of the Carpathian military district with a strong support of air units. Other Soviet divisions came from the territory of Germany towards Prague and Pilsen. Soviet troops of the group "South" and the 8th Hungarian division came from north-west Hungary towards Bratislava. Hungarian units occupied south-west Slovakia. One part of Soviet units of the 38th troop came from the east, through Vyšné Nemecké towards Prešov, Poprad and Trenčín. Another part came through Veľké Kapušany towards Košice and Zvolen. This part came together with one Bulgarian regiment, which occupied the Sliač airport. The invading troops occupied all strategic points of Czechoslovakia (government, Party buildings, communication centres and others) in just 30 hours.

Political decision-making on the destiny of our country after the invasion was left to Moscow, where on the 23rd of August negotiations started on the political solutions, after the failure of a collaborative government. Brezhnev, Alexej Kosygin, Nikolaj Podgornyj and others participated in these negotiations on the Soviet side, the Czechoslovak side was represented by those released from internment—Dubček, Černik, Smrkovský, Šimon and Špack, together with them Ludvik Svoboda, Biľak, Gustáv Husák, Zdeněk Mlynář. The Soviets insisted the final document would state that the Czechoslovak leadership accepted enemy activities, and that Dubček had not heeded the frequent Soviet warnings about the risk of counterrevolution Czechoslovakia faced. The final document with the title 'Moscow Protocol' was a Soviet dictation. It contained measures that Dubček had to perform in the politics of media, in the issues of the political programme, in foreign policy and others. Soviet representatives of the Ministry of Foreign Affairs (Katushev and others) came to

Czechoslovakia to control the fulfilment of the Moscow Protocol. This protocol was signed by all Czechoslovak representatives who participated in the negotiation, except F. Kriegel and it was a top secret document until the fall of the communist regime.

Gustáv Husák, Vice President of the Czechoslovak government, played an important role in the Moscow negotiations, sent to Moscow by the Presidency of the Central Committee KSČ and the Presidency of the Slovak National Council, to request the release from internment of Dubček and others and to request the departure of the occupation troops. The fast rise of G. Husák started in Moscow. He replaced V. Biľak as 1st Secretary of the Central Committee KSS and became a supporter of Soviet interests. The Soviet leadership considered as cowardice Indra and Biľak failure to form a workers'-farmers' government of the representatives of the so-called 'healthy powers' and decision instead to hide out at the Soviet Embassy in Prague. However, this accusation of cowardice quickly disappeared from the Soviet evaluation. In the period of normalization, V. Biľak represented an important Soviet supporter and probably the control of the 1st Secretary, later Secretary General of the Central Committee KSČ, G. Husák.

V. Biľak explained the fast rise of G. Husák during the Moscow negotiations at the end of August 1968 by the fact that during a break in the negotiations, there was an unofficial conversation between Brezhnev and Husák.[271] During this conversation, Husák reportedly promised to enforce the Soviet requirements and declare the Congress of the Communist Party in Prague-Vysočany void and postpone the Slovak Congress KSS. Brezhnev appreciated Husák's helpfulness in enforcing the Soviet requirements. G. Husák was elected during the Slovak Congress for 1st Secretary KSS and under his leadership started the process of normalization in Slovakia as well as in Czechoslovakia. Its content was to stop the process of reformation and return to the conditions of the regime before the year 1968.

Operation 'Danube' was a military operation and ended with the occupation of Czechoslovakia in 30 hours from its beginning. Negotiations on the legalization of the invasion began, contained in the Moscow Protocol and Agreement on Temporary Stay of Soviet armies in the territory of Czechoslovakia.

---

271 Michal Macháček, *Gustáv Husák* (Praha: Vyšehrad, 2017), 403.

This agreement contained an article that Soviet troops would be positioned in the territory of Czechoslovakia without setting the time period or a secret protocol for the treaty.

The conditions of positioning of the Soviet troops in the territory of Czechoslovakia were debated in the meeting of the Warsaw Pact with the participation of the leaders of the countries that had participated in the invasion. The meeting was held on 27th September in Moscow.

The basis for the negotiation was the opinion of the Soviet leadership presented by Brezhnev. He stated the invasion of the troops was inevitable and it was performed in time because the counterrevolution was active.[272] After this meeting, the Czechoslovak delegation (Dubček, Černík, Husák) visited Moscow to negotiate with the Soviet representatives the positioning of the Soviet troops. Dubček said during the meeting that the Czechoslovak side was prepared to offer accommodation for 70–80 thousand soldiers and proposed to return to the negotiation of the departure of Soviet troops.

The basis of the treaty between Czechoslovakia and the Soviet Union on the conditions of a temporary stay of Soviet troops in the territory of Czechoslovakia was the Soviet design debated with the Czechoslovak delegation during the visit to Moscow on the 3rd and 4th of October. The treaty of 15 articles was signed by Prime Ministers Černík and Kosygin and—after being approved by parliament—ratified on the 18th October by the President of the Republic. A secret protocol was approved together with the treaty, this protocol stated that there would be 70,000 Soviet soldiers deployed in the territory of Czechoslovakia.

After Brezhnev's death, a document emerged reproaching the operation 'Danube' for two mistakes—the positioning of heavy machinery in the town squares and in narrow streets of large towns during the first days of occupation could have led to heavy losses and it influenced the patriotism of Czechoslovak citizens. The second mistake was a bad coordination of the military operations with the performance of political aims and insufficiencies of the Soviet propaganda[273].

---

272 Jitka Vondrová and Jaromir Navrátil, *Mezinárodní souvislosti československé kríze 1967–1970. Červenec-srpen 1968. Díl 4/2, sv. 2.* Praha—Brno: ÚSD AV ČR v nakladatelství Doplněk, 1996, 77.

273 Quotation from *Izvestija*, August 22, 1995.

The invasion and deployment of Soviet troops prevented further reforms and the performance of the programme of 'socialism with a human face'. With the help of local adversaries of the reform, the neo-Stalinist regime from the period before January 1968 was restored and the representatives of the reforms were considered enemies of Socialism and persecuted.

Soviet political and military leadership considered the operation 'Danube' successful and it served as a model. During the 70's and 80's, it was taught as such in Soviet military schools. Its aim was described as the support of a particular ideological system using operative-strategic troops. The operation was more a special than a military action focused on the 'stabilisation' of the political regime in Czechoslovakia.

The fall of the Communist regimes of the Soviet bloc at the end of the 1980s caused a re-evaluation of the operation 'Danube' and its consequences within the occupation. On the 3rd of December 1989, Czechoslovak Federal government approved a statement on the invasion of the Warsaw Pact armies on 21st August 1968 as a breach of international law and of relations between sovereign countries. During the meeting of Mikhail Gorbachev with the Czechoslovak representatives Ladislav Adamec (Prime Minister of the Federal government) and Karol Urbánek (new representative of Central Committee KSČ after Miloš Jakeš) on the 4th of December 1989, a resolution was approved that the invasion was against the norms of relations between sovereign countries. The meeting of representatives of the member states of the Warsaw Pact—the Soviet Union, Bulgaria, Hungary, Germany, Poland and Romania (the last of which did not participate in the invasion)—culminated in a joint statement that the Warsaw Pact troops' invasion on the 21st of August 1968 had been illegal, unfounded and erroneous. This statement by the member states of the Warsaw Pact also produced a Treaty on the temporary deployment of Soviet troops in Czechoslovakia from the 18th October 1968. Relations between Czechoslovakia and the Soviet Union were to acquire a new form based on the principle of equality and non-intervention in internal affairs. This was agreed by the Czechoslovak president Václav Havel with the Soviet president Mikhail Gorbachev during an official visit to Moscow on the 26th of February, 1990. Apart from a declaration of the principles of mutual relations with a correction of the errors from the past, the Ministers of Foreign Affairs Eduard Shevardnadze and Jiří Dienstbier signed a treaty on the departure of the Soviet troops from Czechoslovakia in three phases until the

30th of June, 1991. The signing of the protocol of the governments of the USSR and the CSSR on the 26th of June, 1991 was the official end of the stay of Soviet troops and the last soldier left on the 27th of June 1991. After their departure, material and ecological damage was left, as well as the graves of several hundred Czechoslovak citizens who lost their lives in the invasion and occupation.

10
The Prague Spring and the Warsaw Pact Invasion of Czechoslovakia in 1968 as Reflected in the "Western" Historiography[274]

Jakub Drábik

Because of the sheer destructiveness of the rivalry between the two Superpowers of the First and Second World and the general level of tension in the Third World, Cold War studies and historiography have tended to focus on armed conflicts.[275] This is not the case, however, with the Prague Spring and its aftermath. Since August 21–22, 1968, when literally overnight the Czechoslovak experiment was transformed from living reality to history, the so-called Prague Spring and the subsequent occupation of Czechoslovakia by the combined forces of the Warsaw Pact have not ceased to inspire historical research and public debate.

The response of the world's media was immediate. The very morning after the invasion, the British *Guardian* reported that:

> after 50 years communism still means, in Soviet eyes, the rule of the tank and the jack-boot. And after a decade in which, all over the world, hopes had risen that civilised relations between nations might at last become the rule, the Russian leadership has retreated into its old imperialism. The aim of the reformist movement in Czechoslovakia was simple. It was to bring elementary civilities and freedoms into the Socialist way of life.[276]

Condemnation of the invasion was almost universal, including by three Communist states (one of them, Romania, was a member of the Warsaw Pact). A UN Security Council resolution also sought to condemn the action, but the draft resolution was blocked, not surprisingly, by the USSR.[277]

---

274 This is an updated and slightly amended version of the paper previously published in Historický časopis, vol. 68, No. 4/2020, p. 693–722.
275 Federico Romero, "Cold war historiography at the crossroads," *Cold War History* 14, no. 4 (2014): 693.
276 Editorial, "Jackboots again over Eastern Europe," *The Guardian*, August 22, 1968.
277 Richard Goodman, "The invasion of Czechoslovakia: 1968," *The International Lawyer* 4, no. 1 (1969): 43.

In addition to causing considerable disquiet among national governments, journalists and academics, the invasion also stirred up trouble within the Communist movement worldwide. Influential Communist parties like those of Italy and Spain denounced the 'occupation'; the response of others, such as the Communist party of Greece, was divided. The French Communist party's condemnation of the invasion—probably the first time in its history it had publicly criticised any action by the Soviets—was rapidly retracted through the party's support of the subsequent "normalisation".[278] A CIA memorandum of September 9 1968 concluded that the reaction of Communist parties across the world had "clearly shown that the CPSU [Communist Party of the Soviet Union] can no longer exact the support of the large majority of the parties at the cost of their own interests."[279]

The Prague Spring and its quashing by soviet tanks was not only an important event in Czech and Slovak national history; it also had a wider, global reach comparable to the signing of the Munich Agreement in 1938, the coup d'état of 1948, and the Velvet Revolution of 1989, and piqued the interest of many scholars, journalists and ordinary people, and of course historians. It is no surprise, then, that the Prague Spring of 1968 is one of the best known and most thoroughly researched events in Czechoslovak history. It seems only appropriate, therefore, especially following the fiftieth anniversary of the event in 2018, to establish the current "state of play".

The essay does not seek to provide a complete list of works concerning the Prague Spring and the occupation of 1968—such a task would be impossible. When the Canadian historian Gordon Skilling published his *Czechoslovakia's Interrupted Revolution*, he counted over 600 books that dealt with the subject.[280] That was in 1976, over 40 years ago, and the sheer volume of literature on the subject is now larger and even more overwhelming. Instead, the essay will focus on the most significant works and seek to capture and analyse the main trends in the research into and writing about this event. It will focus on the Western historiography—

---

278 George Ross, "Party decline and changing party systems: France and the French communist party," *Comparative Politics* 25, no. 1 (1992): 48.
279 Central Intelligence Agency, *Intelligence Memorandum: World Communist Reaction to the Invasion of Czechoslovakia*, 9 September 1968. CIA archives, FOIA Collection, doc. 0000126786. https://www.cia.gov/library/readingroom/document/0000126876
280 Gordon Skilling, *Czechoslovakia's Interrupted Revolution* (Princeton: Princeton University Press, 1976), 5.

especially works written in English—as that contribution to the scholarship is the most numerous and, arguably, the most influential. It will also pay brief attention to the work of German, Italian and French historians.

***

Early works

Fascination with the events that took place in Czechoslovakia in 1968 started shortly after the invasion; the first academic works appeared only months later. As early as December, the University of New York ran a conference called "The Impact of the Czechoslovak Events on Current International Relations"; the papers were published in 1970 in a volume entitled *Czechoslovakia Intervention and Impact*.[281] Its authors speculated about what prompted the USSR to intervene: Jan F. Triska saw the primary cause in economic failures; William Zartman stressed the Soviets' fear that the Czechoslovak Communist party had lost control. Other essays focused on the lack of response by the United States of America or the impact of the invasion on NATO. There are also some interesting comparisons with the Soviet intervention in Hungary and activities in Romania. Although some important points were made, much of the argument lacked the solidity of the events themselves. In an article published in 1969, Richard Goodman assessed the legality of the Soviet action and criticised the less than enthusiastic response of the West and the United Nations. Goodman concluded that the West's failure to act appeared to be an attempt to avoid direct involvement in Czechoslovakia in the hope that the Soviets would not exert any more pressure on their vassal.[282]

The first books of note also appeared in double-quick time. January 1969 saw the publication of the *Czech Black Book*,[283] compiled by Czechoslovak historians from the Institute of the History of the Czechoslovak

---

281 William Zartman, ed., *Czechoslovakia Intervention and Impact* (New York: New York University Press, 1970).
282 Goodman, "The invasion of Czechoslovakia," 78–79.
283 Robert Littell, ed., *The Czech Black Book: An Eyewitness, Documented Account of the Invasion of Czechoslovakia* (New York: Frederick A. Praeger, 1969; London: Pall Mall, 1969). The English version omitted some of the material that appeared in the original Czech version.

Academy of Sciences and first published in Czech.[284] At 500 pages long, this monster of a book was never available to buy in full in Czechoslovakia but was reproduced in samizdat form across the country. The English version—it was also published in German as *Das tschechische Schwarzbuch*[285]—was edited by Robert Littell and published as a response to the "White Book" in which the Soviet invaders had sought to justify their actions.[286] *The Czech Black Book* is a collection of documents intended as the raw material for history and presented in the form of an hour-by-hour account of the invasion, the initial impact of the military intervention, and the days that followed, up to the time the delegation of the Czechoslovak government returned from the negotiations in Moscow. The work does not seek to analyse the events, only to record what happened.

The Czech Black Book was followed in May 1969 by Harry Schwartz's *Prague's 200 Days: The Struggle for Democracy in Czechoslovakia*.[287] Schwartz attempted a more coherent analysis of the situation but his journalistic approach over-dramatised events and created an almost romantic view of the aspirations of the democratic Czechoslovak spirit and of its ruthless destruction by Soviet tanks. He failed, however, to explore and explain the complex topic of the liberalisation of Communism in Czechoslovakia and left almost all the major questions unanswered.

In *The Czechoslovak Crisis 1968*,[288] Robert Rhodes attempted an explanation of the background to the Prague Spring. Although his analysis was deeper and more comprehensive than that of Schwartz, he failed to assess in any way successfully the domestic developments that had been taking place in Czechoslovakia from January 1968, when Dubček was named the Communist party's First Secretary, to the day of the invasion. He ignored important details concerning the history of the Czechoslovak

---

284 Josef Macek et al., *Sedm pražských dnů 21.–27. srpen 1968* (Praha: Historický ústav CSAV, 1968).

285 Günther Wagenlehner and Werner von Marx, eds., *Das tschechische Schwarzbuch—Die Tage vom 20. bis 27. August 1968 in Dokumenten und Zeugenaussagen* (Stuttgart: Seewald Verlag, 1969).

286 First published in Soviet *Pravda* on 22 August and subsequently as a brochure. It was full of disinformation and claimed there was a "counter-revolution in the air".

287 Harry Schwartz, *Prague's 200 Days: The Struggle for Democracy in Czechoslovakia* (New York: Frederick A. Praeger, 1969).

288 Robert Rhodes James, *The Czechoslovak Crisis 1968* (London: Weidenfeld & Nicolson, 1969).

Communist party, such as the fact that it was a legal party with a considerable membership during the interwar years and was equally strong after the war. Supposedly an academic work, Rhodes's book contains some serious omissions.

Among other noteworthy books published in 1969 was Isaac D. Levine's *Intervention. The Causes and Consequences of the Invasion of Czechoslovakia*, which made much of the White House's admission that there would be no change in its policy towards the USSR after the invasion of Czechoslovakia.[289] Robin Remington gathered together a valuable collection of documents, including the "Action Programme" and "2000 Words"; some important documents are missing, however.[290]

Thus, the late 1960s saw a minor boom in works dedicated to the Prague Spring and the invasion of 1968.[291] And not only in English. The Czechs-in-exile quarterly *Svědectví* ("Evidence"), published in Paris since 1956, dedicated three of its 1969 editions (34, 35 and 36) to a systematic presentation of documents and commentaries relating to the events of 1968. Pavel Tigrid, one of the most important figures in Czech journalism in exile and a founder of *Svědectví*, published his *Le Printempts de Prague*,[292] and a work that analysed Dubček's reforms and his fall.[293] Numerous other books were published in French[294] and Italian.[295]

---

[289] Isaac Levine, *Intervention. The Causes and Consequences of the Invasion of Czechoslovakia* (Philadelphia: McKay, 1969), 70.

[290] Robin Remington, ed., *Winter in Prague: Documents on Czechoslovak Communism in Crisis* (Cambridge: MIT Press, 1969).

[291] Other works worth mentioning include Zbynek Zeman, *Prague Spring: A Report on Czechoslovakia 1968* (London: Penguin, 1969); Philip Windsor and Adam Roberts, *Czechoslovakia, 1968: Reform, Repression, and Resistance* (London: Columbia University Press—Institute for Strategic Studies, 1969).

[292] Pavel Tigrid, *Le printempts de Prague* (Paris: Editions du Seuil, 1968).

[293] Pavel Tigrid, *La chute irresistible d'Alexander Dubček* (Paris: Calmann-Levy, 1969). Later published in Italian as *Così finì Alexander Dubček* (Milano: Edizioni del Borghese, 1970) and in English as *Why Dubček Fell* (London: MacDonald, 1971).

[294] For example, French journalist Michel Salomon wrote *Prague: la revolution etranglee, janvier–aout 1968* (Paris: Laffont, 1968); other works include Jacques Marcelle, *Le deuxieme coup de Prague* (Brussels: Editions Vie Ouvriere, 1968); the communist Pierra Daix wrote *Journal de Prague, decembre 1967–septembre 1968* (Paris: Juillard, 1968); the Trotskyist Pierre Brouté wrote *Le Printemps des peuples commence a Prague* (Paris: La Vérité Trotskyste, 1968).

[295] For example, Alexander Dubček, *Il nuovo corso in Cecoslovacchia* (Roma: Editori riuniti, 1968); Pavel Tigrid, *Praga 1948–Agosto 1968* (Milano: Jaca Book, 1968); Arrigo

Another key figure of the Prague Spring was Pavel Kohout. Kohout was expelled from the Communist party and his works were subject to strict censorship. He therefore switched to publishing in German, including, in 1969, a book dedicated to the events of 1968.[296] Přemysl Pitter, the Protestant preacher and radical pacifist, who had had to emigrate in the early 1950s, also published a book in German in which he approached the events from the perspective of the country's spiritual and religious traditions.[297] There were also first attempts at a more academic approach, which could be seen in *Viva Dubček: Reform und Okkupation in der CSSR*[298] and a collection of documents collected and edited by Hanswilhelm Haefs, although the majority of the documents here are not full.[299] The Italian Communist Gianlorenzo Pacini also showed sympathy towards Dubček's reforms in his book *La svolta di Praga e la Cecoslovacchia invasa*.[300]

Several books concerning the economic aspect of the reforms were published by Czech authors and translated into English. Some of these works were briefly available in Czechoslovakia.[301] Among them, those by Ota Šik, the man behind the New Economic Model (economy liberalization plan), stand out as an interesting contribution to an understanding of the thinking behind the reforms.[302] Jiří Pelikán—who organised the

---

Bongiorno, *L'utopia bruciata* (Milano: Sugar, 1968). See also the translation of the Action Programme of the Czechoslovak Communist Party (published before the invasion itself): *La via cecoslovacca al socialismo. Il programma d'azione e il progetto di statuto del Partito comunista di Cecoslovacchia* (Roma: Editori riuniti, 1968).

296 Pavel Kohout, *Tagebuch eines Konterrevolutioniirs* (Luzern: Biicher Verlag, 1969).

297 Přemysl Pitter, *Geistige Revolution im Herzen Europas* (Zurich: Rotapfel Verlag, 1968).

298 Adolf Müller and Christian Schmidt-Häuer, *Viva Dubček: Reform und Okkupation in der ČSSR* (Köln: Kiepaenheuer und Witsch, 1968).

299 Hanswilhelm Haefs, ed., *Die Ereignisse in der Tschechoslowakei vom 27.6.1967 bis 18.10.1968: Ein dokumehtarischer Bericht* (Bonn: Siegler, 1969).

300 Gianlorenzo Pacini, *La svolta di Praga e la Cecoslovacchia invasa* (Rome: Samona and Savelli, 1969).

301 Radovan Richta et al., *Civilization at the Crossroads* (New York: International Arts and Sciences Press, 1968); Josef Goldman and Karel Kouba, *Economic Growth in Czechoslovakia: An Introduction to the Theory of Economic Growth under Socialism, Including an Experimental Application of Kalecki's Model of Czechoslovak Statistical Data* (White Plains: International Arts and Sciences Press Inc. 1966, and especially the later edition from 1969); Radoslav Selucký, *Czechoslovakia: The Plan That Failed* (London: Nelson, 1970).

302 Ota Šik, *Plan and Market Under Socialism* (White Plains: International Arts and Sciences Press Inc, 1967). There were also French and German translations—see references

resistance among journalists after the invasion in 1968, and fled the country in 1969—edited the proceedings and materials of the Communist Party of Czechoslovakia's 14th Party Congress, which was held secretly in a factory in Prague the day after troops entered the city.[303] These documents contain important data on the planned reforms and "what might have been".[304]

The first high-quality studies

Judging by the number of books that continued to be published, interest in the events of 1968 remained high into the early 1970s.[305] By now, however, the focus has shifted towards a more scholarly analysis and away from the purely journalistic description characteristic of many works from late 1960s. One of the first highly significant publications from the later period is a book by Grey Hodnett and Peter J. Potichnyj concerned with the link between the events in Czechoslovakia and developments taking place in the border areas of Soviet Ukraine. In *The Ukraine and the Czechoslovak Crisis*, the authors indicated that Soviet authorities had a good overview of the situation in eastern Czechoslovakia, which included attitudes among the general public and contact between some Czechoslovak communist

---

in Gordon Skilling, "Thaw and freeze-up: Prague 1968," *International Journal* 25, no. 1 (1969): 192–201.

303 Jiří Pelikán, ed., *The Secret Vysočany Congress. Proceedings and Documents of the Extraordinary Fourteenth Congress of the Communist Party of Czechoslovakia, 22 August 1968* (London: Allen Lane, 1971). First published in French as Jiří Pelikán, ed., *Le congres clandestin* (Paris: Seuil, 1969).

304 Gordon Skilling, "Reform aborted: Czechoslovakia in retrospect," *International Journal* 28, no. 3 (1973): 440.

305 The many works published in the 1970s include E. J. Czerwinski and Jaroslaw Piekalkiewicz, eds., *The Soviet Invasion of Czechoslovakia: Its Effects on Eastern Europe* (New York: Praeger Publishers, Inc., 1972); Jaroslaw Piekalkiewicz, *Public Opinion Polling in Czechoslovakia, 1968–1969: Results and Analysis of Surveys Conducted during the Dubcek Era* (New York: Praeger, 1972); Bennett Kovrig, *The Myth of Liberation: East-Central Europe in U.S. Diplomacy and Politics Since 1941* (Baltimore: Johns Hopkins University Press, 1973); Andrzej Korbonski, "Bureaucracy and interest groups in Communist societies: The case of Czechoslovakia," *Studies in Comparative Communism* 4, no. 1 (1971): 57–79; Benjamin Page, *The Czechoslovak Reform Movement 1963-1968: A Study in the Theory of Socialism* (Amsterdam: B. R. Grüner, 1973); and one of the first biographies of Alexander Dubček in English: William Shawcross, *Dubček* (London: Weidenfeld & Nicolson, 1970).

party members in and around Prešov and Soviet security services. No clear conclusions are drawn, but the authors do suggest that information collected from the region had some impact on the final decision to intervene in the country.[306]

The beginning of the 1970s finally produced some high-quality historical studies of the period, some of which remain relevant today. One of the first of these was Galia Golan's well-researched *The Czechoslovak Reform Movement* (1971), which analysed the political changes that took place in Czechoslovakia in depth and traced the liberalisation of various spheres of Czechoslovak society, from the economy to culture, analysing them chronologically from the first small steps at the beginning of the 1960s right up to the transformation of the liberalising tendencies into a mass movement and its suppression in August 1968. She also noted the differences between Czech and Slovak perceptions of what was more important (democratisation vs. federalisation) and the controversies and problems between the two nations. The book includes an extensive bibliography that contains numerous primary sources. It thus became a key resource for studying Czechoslovakia for years to come.[307]

Other important works published in 1971 include Vladimir Kusin's *The Intellectual Origins of the Prague Spring*[308] and Ivan Sviták's *The Czechoslovak Experiment: 1968-1969*.[309] Both authors lived in Czechoslovakia throughout the period and are therefore also protagonists in their own narratives. The Marxist philosopher Sviták had been one of the most radical reformers and vocal advocates of democratic socialism in Czechoslovakia in the 1960s, urging complete transformation of the 'totalitarian dictatorship': real democracy, not simply the 'democratisation' of the party. After the invasion, Sviták was stripped of his citizenship, but instead of

---

306 Grey Hodnett and Peter Potichnyj, *The Ukraine and the Czechoslovak Crisis* (Canberra: Australian National University, 1970).
307 See also her analysis of Antonín Novotný's rule: Galia Golan, "Antonin Novotny: The sources and nature of his power," *Canadian Slavonic Papers* 14, no. 3 (1972): 421–441.
308 Vladimír Kusín, *The Intellectual Origins of the Prague Spring: The Development of Reformist Ideas in Czechoslovakia 1956-1967* (New York: Cambridge University Press, 1971).
309 Ivan Sviták, *The Czechoslovak Experiment: 1968-1969* (New York: Columbia University Press, 1971). First published in German as Ivan Sviták, *Verbotene Horizonte, Prag zwischen zwei Wintern* (Freiburg im Breisgau: Rombach, 1969).

serving a jail term, he chose to emigrate.[310] In his book, which serves as a document of the intellectual history of the period, he took a broad view of Dubček's experiment, seeing it not only as a challenge to Communism and Soviet supremacy in Central and Eastern Europe but also as a challenge to Russian supremacy within the Soviet Union. Kusín, on the other hand, looked to history to explain what lay behind the liberalisation movement. He concluded that although the 1948 coup d'état destroyed democratic structures in the country, the tradition lived on and once circumstances allowed it (that is, after Khrushchev's famous speech of 1956, and when the Czechoslovak economy was in serious trouble in the early 1960s), a gradual emancipation from Stalinism took place. Overall, the book struck a balance with Western discussions that had tended to downplay the contribution of academics to the 'democratisation' process.[311]

Like Sviták, Jaroslav Krejčí also emigrated after the invasion, to the United Kingdom. His important *Social Change and Stratification in Post-War Czechoslovakia* (1972),[312] represented the first serious analysis of sociological changes in Czechoslovakia after the Second World War. Perhaps even more significant than Krejčí's analysis, however, was Kusin's second entry to the debate. In *Political Groupings in the Czechoslovak Reform Movement* (1972),[313] Kusin made a detailed investigation of the various political groups which had emerged in the 1960s in Czechoslovakia and which made 1968 possible. His focus is on intellectuals, writers and artists, but he also paid close attention to workers and the trade union movement. Another work of Ota Šik's also appeared in 1972: *Czechoslovakia: The Bureaucratic Economy*.[314] These were the very first accounts that allowed Western academics and people at large to understand the nature of Czechoslovakia's movement for 'democratisation', although as works written by

---

310 For a more detailed study on Ivan Sviták, see Roman Kanda, "Ivan Sviták a pražské jaro 1968," *Filosofický časopis* 66, no. 4 (2018): 543–565.
311 See also Gordon Skilling's analysis of Golan and Kusin's work in Skilling, "Reform aborted," 432–435.
312 Jaroslav Krejčí, *Social Change and Stratification in Post-War Czechoslovakia* (London: Macmillan, 1972).
313 Vladimir Kusin, *Political Groupings in the Czechoslovak Reform Movement* (New York: Columbia University Press, 1972).
314 Ota Šik, *Czechoslovakia: The Bureaucratic Economy* (White Plains: International Arts and Sciences Press Inc, 1972).

émigrés, they provided not only a great deal of detailed information but also a certain degree of subjectivity.

Other important contributions appeared soon after the books by Krejčí and Kusin. Of those published in 1973, two stand out: Galia Golan's *Reform Rule in Czechoslovakia: The Dubček Era, 1968–1969*,[315] and a short article by Gordon Skilling which offered a critical evaluation of the scholarly literature on the subject.[316] Golan's book, received by many reviewers as the "best scholarly study so far",[317] was the result of detailed research of the available evidence. One of Golan's many observations was that while the pre-1968 debate represented a kind of "revolution from above", the events of 1968 created a mass movement which received support from almost all strata of the Czechoslovak populace. Kusin helped to organize a conference on Dubček's reforms in the summer of 1971 at the University of Reading, which resulted in the publication of an edited volume of papers in 1973. Several Czech authors participated—Miloslav Bernášek, Dušan Havlíček, Ivan Bystřina and Karel Jezdinský—but no Slovaks.[318] Jiří Pelikán published an interesting collection of documents which indicated that neither the "resistance" nor the more general opposition in Czechoslovakia had ceased since occupation.[319]

Alongside the works by Galia Golan and Vladimir Kusin, Gordon Skilling's 'classic' work *Czechoslovakia's Interrupted Revolution* was arguably among the most comprehensive and well-researched works of the period, and at 925 pages, clearly aspired to be the definitive work on the subject.[320] Dividing his research into six parts, Skilling analysed with scholarly precision almost every aspect of the reform movement. The first two parts deal with the period before 1968. While other authors generally highlighted the Czechoslovaks' proud tradition of democracy, Skilling was

---

315 Galia Golan, *Reform Rule in Czechoslovakia: The Dubček Era, 1968–1969* (Cambridge: Cambridge University Press, 1973).
316 Skilling, "Reform aborted," 431–445.
317 See, for example, B. Kymlicka, "Reviewed Work: Reform Rule in Czechoslovakia: The Dubcek Era, 1968–1969 by GALIA GOLAN," *Canadian Slavonic Papers* 16, no. 2 (1974): 309.
318 Vladimir Kusin, ed., *The Czechoslovak Reform Movement, 1968* (London: International Research Documents, 1973).
319 Jiří Pelikan, *Ici Prague—l'opposition interieure* (Paris: Seuil, 1973).
320 Gordon Skilling, *Czechoslovakia's Interrupted Revolution* (Princeton: Princeton University Press, 1976).

more sceptical and suggested that short periods of democracy were outweighed by centuries of dominance by absolutist regimes. The communist party itself, a legal body, was part of this Czechoslovak interwar democratic tradition after all. Skilling claimed that it was a crisis of the system created by communist party which had caused the foundation and strengthening of the reform movement, and not some vague notions about democracy and democratic tradition. Fully three-quarters of the book are dedicated to the events of 1968, placed in chronological order but also in their historical context. Importantly, however, some of the Skilling's conclusions—such as his classification of the 'conservative' and 'moderate' wings of the party, and his placing of individual members of the party within these categories—turned out to be misleading and in need of reconsideration by later academic research.

The first studies dealing with various related matters also appeared in the 1970s: Richard B. Craig and David J. Gillespie considered the Yugoslav reaction to the invasion;[321] Hana Beneš analysed the Czech literature on the subject;[322] George Klein wrote an interesting comparative study of the role of ethic politics in the Czechoslovak crisis of 1968 and the Yugoslav crisis of 1971;[323] Vladimir Fišera edited an important volume on workers' councils in Czechoslovakia.[324] Czechoslovak post-1968 émigrés made further contributions, both in English and German;[325] Jiří Kosta provided German academia with a concise yet comprehensive survey of the postwar economic history of Czechoslovakia with special emphasis on the economic reforms of the late 1960s.[326]

---

[321] Richard Craig and David Gillespie, "Yugoslav reaction to the Czechoslovak liberalization movement and the invasion of 1968," *Australian Journal of Politics & History* 23, no. 2 (1977): 227–238.

[322] Hana Beneš, "Czech literature in the 1968 crisis," *The Bulletin of the Midwest Modern Language Association* 5, no. 2 (1972): 97–114.

[323] George Klein, "The role of ethnic politics in the Czechoslovak crisis of 1968 and the Yugoslav crisis of 1971," *Studies in Comparative Communism* 8, no. 4 (1975): 339–369.

[324] Vladimir Fišera, ed., *Workers' Councils in Czechoslovakia, 1968–1969* (London: Allison and Busby, 1978).

[325] For example, the memoirs of the well-known Czechoslovak chess-player Luděk Pachman were translated into English: Luděk Pachman, *Checkmate in Prague: Memoirs of Luděk Pachman* (London: Faber, 1975).

[326] Jiří Kosta, *Abriss der sozialökonomischen Entwicklung der Tschechoslowakei, 1945–1977* (Frankfurt am Main: Suhrkamp Verlag, 1978).

Along with Skilling, Golan and some others, Robert Dean was among the first to stress the difference between Slovak and Czech perceptions of the reforms, and this was a central theme of his 1973 monograph;[327] Eugen Steiner chose a similar approach.[328] The question of relations between Czechs and Slovaks was especially of interest among Slovak nationalist post-war émigrés, many of whom had collaborated with the Nazi regime. Notable among these was Joseph M. Kirschbaum, who was general secretary of the Hlinka Party and Slovak ambassador to Switzerland during the war.[329] Slovak nationalist exiles claimed that federalisation was the most important outcome of the reform process and that Czech intellectuals were wasting their time discussing economics and ideology. Many were also highly critical of their fellow countryman Dubček, whom they saw as merely an agent of Moscow.[330]

Zdeněk Hejzlar[331] and Vladimír Horský[332]—former members of the Communist Party of Czechoslovakia and active participants in the reformist movement—both expressed the belief that the reform of Communism in Czechoslovakia was possible; both books were published in German. Using theoretical and methodological approaches derived from Max Weber and Ernst Bloch, Horský considered alternatives to the Party's strategy after 1968 and the possibility of saving at least some parts of the reform programme. The British political scientist and historian Archibald Haworth Brown also rose to prominence in the 1970s, writing widely on Soviet and Communist politics.[333] Another major scholar interested in the

---

327 Robert Dean, *Nationalism and Political Change in Eastern Europe: The Slovak Question and the Czechoslovak Reform Movement* (Denver: University of Denver Press, 1973).
328 Eugen Steiner, *The Slovak Dilemma* (Cambridge: Cambridge University Press, 1973).
329 See, for example, Joseph Kirschbaum, *Die Slowakie in der Nachkriegsentwicklung der Tschecho-Slowakei* (Köln: Matus Cernak Institute, 1971).
330 Stephen Glejdura, "Slovak-Soviet relations 1939–1971," in *Slovakia in 19th and 20th Centuries: Proceedings of the Conference on Slovakia Held During the General Meeting of the Slovak World Congress on June 17–18, 1971, in Toronto*, ed. Joseph Kirschbaum (Toronto: Slovak World Congress, 1973), 265–280.
331 Zdeněk Hejzlar, *Reformkommunismus: Zur Geschichte der Kommunistischen Partei der Tsechoslowakei* (Köln: Europäische Verlagsanstalt, 1976).
332 Vladimír Horský, *Prag 1968: Systemveränderung und Systemverteidigung* (Stuttgart: Erns Klett Verlag, 1975).
333 Archie Brown dealt with the Czechoslovak crisis in several of his articles, one of the most important being Archie Brown and Gordon Wightman, "Czechoslovakia: Revival

history of Czechoslovakia in general and the events of 1968 in particular was the political scientist David W. Paul, who in the late 1970s and early 1980s produced numerous scholarly works which considered different aspects of Czechoslovak history.[334] In accordance with the historiographical 'cultural turn' in the 1970s away from a positivist epistemology, Paul focused on the political culture in communist Czechoslovakia and raised the question of the nature of the reform movement in 1968.[335]

Western scholarly debates of the 1980s

Interest in the Prague Spring waned in the late 1970s and through the 1980s, but some important contributions were published nonetheless. Academics, journalists and writers began to focus on developments in Czechoslovakia after the invasion and during the so-called normalisation. Kusin defined "normalisation" as the "restoration of authoritarianism in conditions of a post-interventist lack of indigenous legitimacy, carried out under the close supervision of a dominant foreign power which retains the prerogative of supreme arbitration and interpretation but which prefers to work through its domestic agents."[336] Kusin also deals with the huge post-invasion emigration from the country (as many as 170,000 people by 1971), with Charter 77, which he describes and analyses in the context of the growing awareness to human rights, and with the regime's economic achievements; he continued to refine his analysis in several later articles.[337]

---

and retreat," in *Political Culture in Communist States*, ed. Archie Brown and Jack Gray (London: Macmillan, 1977), 159–196.

334 See, for example, David Paul, "The repluralization of Czechoslovak politics in the 1960s," *Slavic Review* 33, no. 4 (1974): 721–740; or his chapter, David Paul "Czechoslovakia's political culture reconsidered," in *Political Culture and Communist Studies*, ed. Archie Brown (London: Palgrave Macmillan, 1984), 137–139; and the shorter work, David Paul, *Czechoslovakia: Profile of a Socialist Republic at the Crossroads of Europe* (Boulder: Westview Press, 1981).

335 This was especially true of David Paul, *The Cultural Limits of Revolutionary Politics: Change and Continuity in Socialist Czechoslovakia* (Boulder: East European Monographs, 1979).

336 Vladimir Kusin, *From Dubček to Charter 77. A Study of "Normalization" in Czechoslovakia 1968–1978* (New York: St. Martin's Press, 1978), 145.

337 See, for example, Vladimir Kusin, "Husák's Czechoslovakia and economic stagnation," *Problems of Communism* 31, no. 3 (1982): 24–37.

In general, Western scholarly debates before 1989 sought various explanations of the origins and nature of normalisation, as well as the roots of Czechoslovak Communism itself. One of the main questions was what had made normalisation possible without its being accompanied by a campaign of terror. Some authors claimed it was the campaign of repression and/or terror that forced Czechs and Slovaks into submission;[338] others such as Kusin claimed that the general public accepted normalisation in exchange for promises of full employment, free health care, an adequate supply of consumer goods, and a decent standard of living. Skilling stressed the domestic roots of the regime, reformation and normalisation;[339] the French historian Jacques Rupnik highlighted the roots of Czechoslovak communism and normalisation among a Czech working class badly affected by the Great Depression of the 1930s.[340] Fred Eidlin attempted to understand 'normalisation' by looking at the first few days after the Soviet invasion. Although he made some interesting points, his book (based on his PhD dissertation of 1980) lacked a sound conceptual and methodological framework and he failed to understand the long-term processes at work and even wrongly supposed that Soviets wanted to stage a rapid normalisation within days of the invasion.[341]

Other authors tried to put the events of the Prague Spring, the August 1968 invasion and the subsequent 'normalisation' in a comparative perspective. American political scientist Zvi Gitelman pointed out similarities and differences between the 'normalisation' in Czechoslovakia after the crushing of the Prague Spring and the "socialist restoration" in Hungary after the 1956 revolution, with a focus on the political elites and the

---

[338] For example, Paul, *Cultural Limits of Revolutionary Politics*; Brown and Wightman, "Czechoslovakia: Revival and retreat," and others.

[339] See his works mentioned above. Also, Gordon Skilling, "Stalinism and Czechoslovak political culture," in *Stalinism: Essays in Historical Interpretation*, ed. Robert Tucker (New York: W. W. Norton, 1977), 257–282.

[340] Jacques Rupnik, "The restoration of the party-state in Czechoslovakia since 1968," in *The Withering Away of the State? Party and State Under Communism*, ed. Leslie Holmes (London: Sage, 1981), 105–125; Jacques Rupnik, "The roots of Czech Stalinism," in *Culture, Ideology and Politics. Essays for Eric Hobsbawm*, ed. Raphael Samuel and Raphael Stedman-Jones (London: Routledge, 1982), 302–319, quoted from the edition published by Routledge in 2016.

[341] Fred Eidlin, *The Logic of "Normalisation": The Soviet Intervention in Czechoslovakia of 21 August 1968 and the Czechoslovak Response* (Boulder: East European Monographs, 1980).

different career paths they followed in their respective countries.[342] A year after Gitelman's article, Włodzimierz Brus, Pierre Kende and Zdeněk Mlynář edited a collective volume which dealt with a wider Eastern European perspective on the 'normalisation' processes in Soviet-dominated Czechoslovakia, Hungary and Poland and featured some important contributions (the chapter on Czechoslovakia was written by Mlynář himself).[343] Jiří Valenta[344] and others[345] followed suit. Judy Batt compared the economic reforms in Czechoslovakia and Hungary;[346] Barbara W. Jancar focused on the women who opposed the regimes in Czechoslovakia and Poland.[347] A lively scholarly discussion of normalisation also appeared in the German historiography.[348]

Another widely discussed topic, prompted in part by the Soviet invasion of Afghanistan in 1979, was the Soviet decision-making processes. Building upon previous scholarship, notably that of Skilling, Kusin and Mlynář, who had all discussed the reasons for the Soviet intervention in Czechoslovakia, Jiří Valenta also analysed Soviet decision-making and concluded that the Soviet decision to intervene in Czechoslovakia was the result of a lengthy and complex process, which he nonetheless sought to explain.[349] The major publication regarding this matter appeared in 1984, when Karen Dawisha, an American expert on Russia, published *The*

---

342 Zvi Gitelman, "The politics of socialist restoration in Hungary and Czechoslovakia," *Comparative Politics* 13, no. 2 (1981): 187–210. Gitelman published another piece of interesting research on public opinion in Czechoslovakia. See Zvi Gitelman, "Public opinion in Czechoslovakia," in *Public Opinion in European Socialist* Systems, ed. Walter Connor (New York: Praeger Publishers, 1977), 83–103.

343 Włodzimierz Brus, Pierre Kende and Zdeněk Mlynář, eds., *"Normalisierungsprozesse" im sowjetisierten Mitteleuropa: Ungarn, Tschechoslowakei, Polen* (Köln: Index, 1982).

344 See, for example, Jiří Valenta, "Revolutionary change, Soviet intervention, and 'Normalization' in East-Central Europe," *Comparative Politics* 16, no. 2 (1984): 127–151.

345 See also, for example, David Paul and Simon Maurice, "Poland today and Czechoslovakia 1968," *Problems of Communism* 30, no. 2 (1981): 25–39.

346 Judy Batt, *Economic Reform and Political Change in Eastern Europe: A Comparison of the Czechoslovak and Hungarian Experiences* (New York: St. Martin's Press, 1988).

347 Barbara Jancar, "Women in the opposition in Poland and Czechoslovakia," in *Women, State and Party in Eastern Europe*, ed. Sharon Wolchik and Alfred Meyer (Durham: Duke University Press, 1985), 64–81.

348 See, for example, Vilém Prečan, *Die Sieben Jahre von Prag, 1969-1976, Briefe und Dokumente aus der Zeit der "Normalisierung"* (Frankfurt am Main: Fischer, 1978).

349 Jiří Valenta, *Soviet Intervention in Czechoslovakia, 1968. Anatomy of a Decision* (Baltimore: The Johns Hopkins University Press, 1979).

Kremlin and the Prague Spring. Dawisha applied the model of foreign policy crisis management developed by Charles Hermann and modified by Michael Breche, made good use of previously unknown or inaccessible documents (for example US intelligence reports) and interviews with active participants in the reform process (such as Zdeněk Mlynář), and explored the motivations of the Soviet leaders in detail.[350]

Other issues were discussed, but not in such detail and usually only by individual scholars.[351] Sharon Wolchik wrote an interesting paper on how the strategies of the Czechoslovak political elites affected women, but across the broader post-war period, not just in 1968.[352] Peter Hruby, the Czech academic and writer who left Czechoslovakia after the 1948 coup d'état, explained the changing role of intellectuals in Czechoslovakia (including Ota Šik and Pavel Kohout), most of whom had embraced a Stalinist variant of communism in the late 1940s and had then become the major proponents of reform.[353] Mark Wright made an analysis of the Czechoslovak political system;[354] the Czech historian Karel Kaplan—who sought

---

350 Karen Dawisha, *The Kremlin and the Prague Spring* (Los Angeles: University of California Press, 1984). See also her earlier work, Karen Dawisha, "The 1968 invasion of Czechoslovakia: Causes, consequences, and lessons for the future," in *Soviet-East European Dilemmas: Coercion, Competition, and Consent*, ed. Karen Dawisha and Philip Hanson (New York: Holmes & Meier, 1981), 9–25.

351 See, for example, Fred Eidlin, "Czechoslovakia: The phony occupation: Normalization in the wake of the 1968 intervention," *Bohemia* 29, no. 2 (1988): 262–279; Kristian Gerner, "De-Stalinisation in Central Europe and the Prague Spring," in *The Soviet Union and Central Europe in the Post-War Era: A Study in Precarious Security*, ed. Kristian Gerner (New York: St. Martin's Press, 1985), 25–40; Chris Harman, "1968: Czechoslovakia—arrested reform," in *Class Struggles in Eastern Europe, 1945–83*, ed. Chris Harman (London: Pluto Press, 1983), 187–211; Robert Hutchings, *Soviet-East European Relations: Consolidation and Conflict, 1968-1980* (Madison: University of Wisconsin Press, 1983), 40–50; Jeffrey Simon, "The invasion of Czechoslovakia, August 1968," in *Cohesion and Dissension in Eastern Europe: Six Crises*, ed. Jeffrey Simon (New York: Praeger, 1983), 42–68; Jurgen Tampke, "Czechoslovakia 1968: A reappraisal," in *The People's Republics in Eastern Europe*, ed. Jurgen Tampke (New York: St. Martin's Press, 1983), 93–113; and others.

352 Sharon Wolchik, "Elite strategy toward women in Czechoslovakia: Liberation or mobilization?" *Studies in Comparative Communism* 14, no. 2–3 (1981): 123–142.

353 Peter Hruby, *Fools and Heroes. The Changing Role of Communist Intellectuals in Czechoslovakia* (Oxford: Pergamon Press, 1980).

354 Mark Wright, "Ideology and power in the Czechoslovak political system," in *Eastern Europe: Political Crisis and Legitimation*, ed. Paul Lewis (London: Croom Helm, 1984), 111–160.

political asylum in West Germany in 1976—addressed political persecution in Czechoslovakia. Kaplan, who had worked on the Committee for Political Rehabilitations during the Prague Spring, was able to access classified Czechoslovak Communist Party (KSČ) documents and used his insider knowledge to good effect in his books.[355] Further works (or their translations) by Czechoslovak émigrés and dissidents appeared,[356] and shortly before the fall of Communism in 1989, *Czechoslovakia: Crossroads and Crises, 1918-88*, a book dedicated to the history of Czechoslovakia, included three chapters that dealt with the events of 1968.[357]

Many of these works from the 1970s and 1980s, especially those of Skilling, Golan, Kusin and Dawisha, are considered 'classics' today. They do indeed retain their value as a ground for research and cannot simply be ignored, but they must be treated with caution as many of the 'facts' and

---

355 Karel Kaplan, *Political Persecution in Czechoslovakia, 1948-1972* (Köln: Index, 1983); see also his later work, Karel Kaplan, *The Communist Party in Power: A Profile of Party Politics in Czechoslovakia* (Boulder: Westview, 1987); on the same topic, see also Robert Evanson "Political repression in Czechoslovakia, 1948-1984," *Canadian Slavonic Papers* 28, no. 1 (1986): 1-21. Kaplan also published a book on the Prague Spring almost immediately after his arrival in the West. See Karel Kaplan, *Winter into Spring: The Czechoslovak Press and the Reform Movement 1963-1968* (New York: Columbia University Press, 1977).

356 For example, the translation of Milan Šimečka's *Obnovení pořádku* with a preface by Zdeněk Mlynář: Milan Šimečka, *The Restoration of Order: The Normalization of Czechoslovakia, 1969-1976* (London: Verso, 1984); or the translation of Zdeněk Mlynář's *Mráz přichází z Kremlu*: Zdeněk Mlynář, *Night Frost in Prague: The End of Humane Socialism* (London: C. Hurst, 1980), also published in German as Zdeněk Mlynář, *Nachtfrost: Das Ende des Prager Frühlings* (Frankfurt am Main: Athenäum, 1988); but also academic works such as Jaroslav Krejčí, "The Prague Spring revisited: A sociological reappraisal," *Czechoslovak and Central European Journal* 8, no. 1-2 (1989): 23-38; Vilém Prečan, "The people—the public—and civil society protagonists in the Prague Spring 1968," *Czechoslovak and Central European Journal* 8, no. 1-2 (1989): 1-22; Zdeněk Suda, "Czechoslovakia: An aborted revolution," in *East Central Europe: Yesterday, Today, Tomorrow*, ed. Milorad Drachkovitch (Stanford: Hoover Institution Press, 1982), 243-265; Milan Švec, "The Prague Spring: 20 years later," *Foreign Affairs* 66, no. 5 (1988): 980-1001; Jiří Pehe, *The Prague Spring: A Mixed Legacy* (Lanham: Freedom House, 1988); and others.

357 Norman Stone and Eduard Strouhal, eds., *Czechoslovakia: Crossroads and Crises, 1918-88* (London: Palgrave Macmillan, 1989). The three chapters are: Milan Hauner, "The Prague Spring—twenty years after" (207-230); Jiří Kosta, "The Czechoslovak economic reform of the 1960s" (231-252); Zdeněk Strmiska, "The Prague Spring as a social movement" (253-267).

especially the interpretations have become obsolete in light of newly found archive material. Although the historiography, right up to the 1990s, was strong on the political, sociological and ideological aspects of the Czechoslovak reform movement and of socialism in general, it suffered from many other problems. First and foremost was the lack of archive material and the limitations caused by such a lack, as well as subjectivity of the available partial material and memoirs. Secondly, it suffered from the mystification of the Prague Spring. Western studies from the early years after the invasion were almost without exception sympathetic to the reformers, although critical notes, especially on the tactics of Dubček and his closest political allies, appeared occasionally.

The Velvet Revolution and beyond

The fall of Communism and the end of Soviet rule in Central and Eastern Europe and the subsequent opening of the archives and the release of many formerly classified documents naturally caused a small boom in the output of Czech and Slovak historians and academics, who were finally free to use primary sources and archives to make sense of their own past. One of the most important undertakings of the early 1990s in Czechoslovakia was the creation of the government commission for the historical analysis of the years 1967–1970 (Odborná komisia vlády ČSFR pre analýzu udalostí rokov 1967–1970), made up of leading Czech and Slovak scholars and historians. In addition to the commission's own detailed report, a vast number of key works appeared in the Czech and Slovak languages during the 1990s. These two countries had their problems, too, however—problems which started as soon as the Velvet Revolution brought an end to Communism in Czechoslovakia. Ideological differences between the various groups had been suppressed in the 1970s and 1980s in service of the common goal of democratisation, but in the run-up to 1989, when it became clear that the collapse of Communism was inevitable, the situation changed. While many former reform Communists still believed in the ideas of the Prague Spring and the possibility of reforming Communism, other groups argued in favour of standard Western-style democracy. Differences also surfaced regarding the various attitudes towards the Prague Spring: for some this remained the ultimate goal; for others it was merely the first step along the road to democracy. The events of 1989 naturally and inevitably caused a change of perspective on the events of 1968 in the Western historiography, and indeed, much of the focus and debate among 'Western' academia shifted from discussion and analysis of the Prague Spring to the more recent Velvet Revolution.

There were nevertheless some important additions in terms of filling in the detail of some of the narrative, but more importantly in terms of interpretation. These new interpretations did not dramatically alter previous understandings and analyses but stressed the validity and importance of some existing interpretations. One of the most important contributions in the 1990s was a pair of studies by Mark Kramer.[358] Kramer showed convincingly that the long-held assumption that the USSR decided to intervene in Czechoslovakia because of Czechoslovak internal issues was not quite accurate, and that the question of the loyalty of the Dubček regime to the foreign and military policies of the USSR was also an important factor.[359] Kramer was also able to analyse some archive material regarding the activities of the KGB and the Czechoslovak secret services.

Early in the 1990s, a number of works sought to set the Prague Spring in a wider context. One of the more interesting of these was published by Michel Oksenberg and Bruce Dickson, and through a new framework for analysing the reforms. The two authors touched on various aspects of the reform process and also took account of Czechoslovak development in the 1960s.[360] Agnes Heller and Ferenc Fehér, two Hungarian political philosophers, attempted to place the Prague Spring within the context of the Cold War and what they called the 'Yalta system'.[361] In their collection of essays written between 1979 and 1989 they considered the development of post-

---

358 For example, Mark Kramer, "New sources on the 1968 Soviet invasion of Czechoslovakia," *Cold War International History Project Bulletin*, no. 2 (1992): 1–19; Mark Kramer, "The Prague Spring and the Soviet invasion of Czechoslovakia: New interpretations," *Cold War International History Project Bulletin*, no. 3 (1993): 1–13.

359 Mark Kramer, "The Czechoslovak crisis and the Brezhnev Doctrine," in *1968. The World Transformed*, ed. Carole Fink, Philipp Gassert and Detlef Junker (Cambridge: Cambridge University Press, 1998), 135–141 (111–171).

360 Michel Oksenberg and Bruce Dickson, "The origins, processes, and outcomes of great political reform," in *Comparative Political Dynamics: Global Research Perspectives*, ed. Dankwart Rustow and Kenneth Erickson (New York: Harper Collins, 1990), 235–261.

361 Agnes Heller and Ferenc Feher, "The place of Prague Spring," in *From Yalta to Glasnost: The Dismantling of Stalin's Empire*, ed. Agnes Heller and Ferenc Feher (London: Blackwell, 1990), 146–161.

war Eastern Europe as one long revolution against the Yalta agreement. Jerome Karabel rather considered it a "revolution of the intellectuals" and compared it with Gorbachev's attempts to reform communism almost 20 years later.[362] Ben Fowkes focused on the defeat of reform Communism within the wider context of the history of the Eastern bloc. He also claimed that in Czechoslovakia, the attempted reform had enjoyed better prospects for success than anywhere else but still failed.[363] Skilling considered the Prague Spring within the wider context of Czechoslovak history, including events such as the Munich crisis of 1938 and the occupation of the Czech lands and the creation of Slovakia in 1939.[364]

New analyses of reactions to the Prague Spring also appeared. Paul A. Kubricht[365] analysed the response of the Johnson administration, while the German historian Hans-Peter Schwarz studied the response of West Germany, particularly in the context of the chancellorship of Kurt Georg Kiesinger (1966–1969).[366] A little later, John G. MacGinn undertook the task of analysing the collective (in)action of NATO during the Prague Spring.[367] What has long been missing is a critical study of the Prague Spring in the wider perspective of Marxist thought, a lack caused predominantly by the political climate of the Cold War and subsequent lack of interest from the West. Some partial results were published by James Satterwhite, who analysed the philosophical and ideological background to the Prague Spring.[368]

---

362 Jerome Karabel, "The revolt of intellectuals: The origins of the Prague Spring and the politics of reform communism," *Research in Social Movements* 18, no. 1 (1995): 93–143.
363 Ben Fowkes, *The Rise and Fall of Communism in Eastern Europe* (Basingstoke: Macmillan; New York: St. Martin's Press, 1993), 118.
364 Gordon Skilling, "Journey to Czechoslovakia: Spring 1968," *Kosmas: Czechoslovak and Central European Journal* 11, no. 1 (Summer 1992): 27–42.
365 Paul Kubricht, "Confronting liberalization and military invasion: America and the Johnson administration respond to the 1968 Prague summer," *Jahrbucher fur Geschichte Osteuropas* 40, no. 2 (1992): 197–212.
366 Hans-Peter Schwartz, "Die Regierung Kiesinger und die Krise in der ČSSR 1968," *Vierteljahrshefte für Zeitgeschichte* 47, no. 2 (1999): 159–186.
367 John McGinn, "The politics of collective inaction. NATO's response to the Prague Spring," *Journal of Cold War Studies* 1, no. 3 (1999): 111–138.
368 See, for example, his book-length study of Marxist revisionism in Eastern Europe: James Satterwhite, *Varieties of Marxist Humanism: Philosophical Revision in Postwar Eastern Europe* (Pittsburgh: University of Pittsburgh Press, 1992), especially the chapter "Czechoslovakia: The philosophical background of the Prague Spring" (130–173); and James

Jaroslav Krejčí elaborated on his previous research and—along with Pavel Machonin, another Czech scholar and one of the most influential Czech sociologists—published an interesting study of social changes in Czechoslovakia, including a sociological analysis of the social stratification of the population before, during and after the Prague Spring.[369] Some important works were also published in German in the 1990s. Lutz Priess, Václav Kural and Manfred Wilke analysed previously unknown documents of the Socialist Unity Party of Germany (*Sozialistische Einheitspartei Deutschlands*, SED) and came to the clear conclusion that the SED rejected the Czechoslovak reforms on the basis of numerous internal studies and subsequently developed its own initiatives to contain and crush the Prague reforms.[370] New biographies of Dubček also appeared. The Lithuanian historian Ina Navazelskis published a short book about the leader of the Prague Spring,[371] but more important was probably Dubček's autobiography.[372] In the autumn of 1996, Karel Bartošek, a Czech historian who was expelled from the Communist Party in 1968 and went into exile in France a few years later, published a study on relations between the French and Czechoslovak communist parties.[373]

The most important works of the 1990s were published in the second half of the decade. Kieran Williams's *The Prague Spring and its Aftermath*[374] remains one of the most valuable contributions to the English historiography. Working with a variety of Czech and, to a lesser degree, Russian sources, Williams set the Prague Spring in the context of the Cold War and made a detailed study of the tensions between Moscow and Prague (and between Brezhnev and Dubček) in the period leading up to the inva-

---

Satterwhite, "Marxist critique and Czechoslovak reform," in *The Road to Disillusion: From Critical Marxism to Postcommunism in Eastern Europe*, ed. Raymond Taras (Armonk: M. E. Sharpe, 1992), 115–134.

369 Jaroslav Krejčí and Pavel Machonin, *Czechoslovakia 1918-92: A Laboratory for Social Change* (New York: St. Martin's Press, 1996).

370 Lutz Priess, Václav Kural and Manfred Wilke, *Die SED und der "Prager Frühling" 1968. Politik gegen einen Sozialismus mit menschlichem Antlitz* (Berlin: Akademie Verlag, 1996).

371 Ina Navazelskis, *Alexander Dubček* (Philadelphia: Chelsea House Publications, 1990).

372 Alexander Dubček, *Hope Dies Last: The Autobiography of Alexander Dubcek*, ed. and trans. Jiří Hochman (New York: Kodansha International, 1993).

373 Karel Bartošek, *Les aveux des archives: Prague—Paris—Prague, 1948-1968* (Paris: Editions du Seuil, 1996).

374 Kieran Williams. *The Prague Spring and its Aftermath. Czechoslovak Politics, 1968-1970.* (Cambridge: Cambridge University Press, 1997)

sion. Williams carefully considered the political failure of the invasion—and especially its consequences—and explained the beginnings of 'normalisation'. He did not succumb to the mythologising of Dubček so prevalent in many previous works and considered critically how he—albeit probably unintentionally—facilitated the restoration of the dictatorial regime.

The other important contribution was the collection of documents compiled by Jaromir Navratil (with a preface by Vaclav Havel and foreword by Gordon Skilling) and published by the CEU Press.[375] His collection presents 140 documents, culled largely from archives in the Czech Republic and Russia, but also from the USA, Hungary, France, Poland and Germany, very few of which had ever been published in English. However, Navrátil's collection concentrated too much on the elite level of communist policies and says very little about the spontaneous creation—though very small—of a civil society in the country. Indeed with a few notable exceptions, most historical analyses in the 1970s, 1980s and 1990s of the events of 1968 focused on communist elites and dissidents and the wider society was generally portrayed merely as forming the background to key events. One of these exceptions was a 1999 study focusing on civil society by Petr Pithart, a Czech political scientist and active participant in the Prague Spring who left the party after the invasion. Pithart did not publish his study in English, however, but in French, in Jackques Rupnik and François Fejtö's edited volume on the Prague Spring.[376] A year earlier, Pithart had published his memoirs in English.[377] Another work worthy of note is Miklos Kun's *Prague Spring, Prague Fall. Blank Spots of 1968* published in 1999.[378] The Hungarian historian collected the testimonies of ten significant former protagonists of the Prague Spring—not just the reformers, but opponents of Dubček and his reforms, including people such as Vasil Biľak, who was one of the major exponents of the hardline wing in the KSČ and also supported the Soviet invasion.

---

375 Jaromír Navrátil et al., *The Prague Spring 1968: A National Security Archive Documents Reader* (Budapest: Central European University Press, 1998).
376 Petr Pithart, "La dualité du Printemps tchéchoslovaque. Société civile et communistes reformateurs," in *Le Printemps tchéchoslovaque 1968*, ed. François Fejtö and Jacques Rupnik (Paris: Editions Complexes, 1999), 77–86.
377 Peter Pithart, *1968—A Memoir of the Prague Spring* (Budapest: Central European University Press, 1998).
378 Miklos Kun, *Prague Spring, Prague Fall. Blank Spots of 1968* (Budapest: Akadémiai Kaido, 1999).

A change of perspective

As we have seen, in the 1990s, some authors—Oksenberg and Dickson, Williams, and others—had already sought to place the developments in Czechoslovakia within the wider context of Soviet foreign policy. This important line in the historiography was then strengthened by Matthew Ouimet, who analysed the Brezhnev Doctrine and dealt with the long-term effect of the Soviet policy in Czechoslovakia on Soviet foreign strategy in general, right up to the dissolution of the USSR.[379] He claimed that the so-called Socialist internationalism was in fact slowly replaced, especially after the Czechoslovak crisis, by national interests and an increasing focus on the domestic stability of the regimes.[380] Gerain Hughes[381] and Saki Ruth Dockrill[382] focused on British policy towards the Eastern bloc and the impact of the Czechoslovak crisis on Britain, adding from the international perspective yet another missing piece to the jigsaw of our understanding of the Prague Spring and its complexity.

Many other aspects of the Prague Spring were described and analysed in more detail and more depth in the 2000s; still others were re-considered. One of these was the often-neglected creation of the embryonic civil society during the Prague Spring and the creation of a mass movement (Golan and others had partially dealt with this subject). In addition to Williams's study,[383] Pat Lyons explored the views of the elite and those abroad in the general public concerning the events associated with the Prague Spring.[384] Another important aspect often neglected by historians

---

379 Matthew Ouimet, *The Rise and Fall of the Brezhnev Doctrine in Soviet Foreign Policy* (Chapel Hill: The University of North Carolina Press, 2003).
380 Similarly, see Robert Jones, *The Soviet Concept of Limited Sovereignty from Lenin to Gorbachev: The Brezhnev Doctrine* (New York: St. Martin's Press, 1990).
381 Geraint Hughes, "British policy towards Eastern Europe and the impact of the 'Prague Spring', 1964–68," *Cold War History* 4, no. 2 (2004): 115–139.
382 Saki Ruth Dockrill, "Defense and detente: Britain, the Soviet Union, and the 1968 Czech crisis," in *The Prague Spring and the Warsaw Pact invasion of Czechoslovakia in 1968*, ed. Günter Bischof, Stefan Karner and Peter Ruggenthaler (Lanham: Lexington Books, 2010), 249–270.
383 Kieran Williams, "The Prague Spring: From elite liberation to mass movement," in *Revolution and Resistance in Eastern Europe: Challenges to Communist Rule*, ed. Kevin McDermott and Matthew Stibbe (Oxford: Berg, 2006), 101–118.
384 Pat Lyons, *Mass and Elite Attitudes during the Prague Spring Era: Importance and Legacy* (Prague: Institute of Sociology, CAS, 2009).

(with some exceptions, such as Karel Bartošek) is that of the impact of the invasion on Communist parties across the world. The most important new perspectives in this area were brought by Maud Bracke, who studied the responses of Western Communist parties to the Czechoslovak crisis of 1968.[385] Her main argument was the need to acknowledge the centrality of "internationalism" for the identity, motivations and strategies of the leaders and militants of Western communist parties and the fact that the Soviet military invasion of Czechoslovakia opened serious further cracks in this concept.[386] Important contributions were also brought by the Spanish historian Giaime Pala.[387]

Many studies of the Prague Spring (Golan, Kusin, Dean, Steiner and others[388]) effectively depicted an oversimplified and erroneous picture of the "split" between Czechs and Slovaks: the "enlightened Czechs" working for democratisation and the "backward Slovaks" concerned only with federalisation.[389] Scott Brown offered a different perspective, which acknowledged that democratisation and federalisation were not mutually exclusive and that many Slovaks linked federalisation to the wider democratisation underway in 1968, regarding one unthinkable without the other.[390] There is, however, still some historiographical debate as to the nature of the link

---

385 Maud Bracke, *Which Socialism? Whose Détente? West European Communism and the Czechoslovak Crisis of 1968* (Budapest: Central European Press, 2007). Also translated into Italian: Maud Bracke, *Quale socialismo, quale distensione? Il comunismo europeo e la crisi cecoslovacca del '68* (Roma: Carocci, 2008).

386 See also her previous work co-written with Thomas Jørgensen: Maud Bracke and Thomas Jørgensen, West European Communism after Stalinism: Comparative Approaches. *EUI Working Paper HEC*, European University Institute, No. 2002/4. Online http://cadmus.eui.eu/bitstream/handle/1814/63/HEC02-04.pdf?sequence=1&isAllowed=y

387 Giaime Pala, "El PSUC y la crisis de Checoslovaquia," *Utopías/Nuestra Bandera*, no. 200 (2004): 67–78. See also the edited volume, Giaime Pala et al., *El inicio del fin del mito soviético. Los comunistas occidentales ante la Primavera de Praga* (Barcelona: El Viejo Topo, 2008).

388 See also, Carol Skalnik Leff, *National Conflict in Czechoslovakia: The Making and Remaking of a State, 1918–1987* (Princeton: Princeton University Press, 1988; reprinted 2014), especially 179–273.

389 For more details also see Adam Hudek, "Problém česko-slovenských vzťahov počas reformného procesu vo vybraných textoch zahraničnej proveniencie." In *Rok 1968 a jeho miesto v našich dejinách*, edited by Miroslav Londák and Stanislav Sikora (Bratislava: Veda and Historický ústav SAV, 2009): 529–542.

390 Scott Brown, "Socialism with a Slovak face: Federalization, democratization, and the Prague Spring," *East European Politics and Societies* 23, no. 3 (2008): 469.

between greater liberalisation of the Czechoslovak political system and greater independence for Slovakia (federalisation) and not all the issues have been settled.

On the 40th anniversary of the Warsaw Pact invasion of Czechoslovakia, an international conference was held at the University of Ottawa, at which academics from all the former Warsaw Pact countries and some North American specialists presented the most up-to-date research on the events of 1968 from their respective countries. Out of the conference came a volume of 16 essays and commentaries—from 18 scholars—compiled and edited by Mark Stolarik.[391]

The role of Alexander Dubček, often idolised in the West, was also subjected to critical analysis. In an essay included in a volume devoted to two key years in the history of Czechoslovakia—1948 and 1968—Mary Heimann (considered a "controversial" historian by many of her Czech and Slovak peers) claimed that Dubček's image as a man of conviction, an idealist and a decent politician was no more than a front and that he successfully used the system to scale the ladder of power.[392] In the same volume, the Slovak political scientist Juraj Marušiak analysed the "soft" version of normalisation and debunked the long-held idea that it had been more moderate in the Slovak part of Czechoslovakia.[393]

The 40th anniversary of the events also saw the culmination of two years of research by the vast Austrian-led international research project, which—under the auspices of the Ludwig Boltzmann Society in Vienna—brought together almost a hundred academics from across the world led by Stefan Kramer. The result was two volumes of essays and documents amounting to almost 3000 pages.[394] Volume One consisted of 70 essays exploring almost every conceivable dimension of the Prague Spring and its end. All 232 of the documents in Volume Two are published in Russian,

---

391 Mark Stolarik, *The Prague Spring and the Warsaw Pact Invasion of Czechoslovakia, 1968. Forty Years Later* (Mundelein: Bolchazy-Carducci, 2010).

392 Mary Heimann, "The scheming apparatchik of the Prague Spring," in *1948 and 1968—Dramatic Milestones in Czech and Slovak History*, ed. Laura Cashman (London: Routledge, 2013), 87–89.

393 Juraj Marušiak, "The normalisation regime and its impact on Slovak domestic policy after 1970," in *1948 and 1968—Dramatic Milestones in Czech and Slovak History*, ed. Laura Cashman (London: Routledge, 2013), 161–181.

394 Stefan Karner et al., *Prager Frühling. Das internationale Krisenjahr 1968* (Köln: Böhlau, 2008).

with a parallel text in German on the facing page, except in the case of American documents, which are reproduced in the original English rather than a German translation. In size and scope, *Prager Frühling. Das internationale Krisenjahr 1968* is the largest such undertaking so far. The conference that took place in April 2008 in New Orleans marked the second stage of the project. The fruit of this was yet another massive tome, this time 'only' 510 pages long, and this time in English: *The Prague Spring and the Warsaw Pact Invasion of Czechoslovakia in 1968*.[395] Both works concluded that the reform of communism in Czechoslovakia, so often lauded as 'socialism with a human face', never had a chance of materialising. To succeed in doing so would have required a fundamental change in Soviet policy, and such a change did not take place until the late 1980s.[396]

German historians produced other important contributions. Konstantin Hermann edited a volume focused on the local perspective of Saxony, then part of East Germany. The authors addressed events such as the Dresden meeting of March 23, 1968, which reached the conclusion that a counter-revolution had broken out in Czechoslovakia and that it was this conclusion that eventually provided the reason for the intervention.[397] The most important contribution to the German historiography in recent years, however, is Martin Schulze Wessel's *Der Prager Frühling: Aufbruch in eine neue Welt*,[398] which introduced an important new perspective to the vast existing literature on the subject. Schulze Wessel focused on the roots of the reform ideas and traced many of them to the rehabilitation programmes of many of the victims of political trials and purges in the 1950s—such as Eduard Goldstücker, who spent almost three years in labour camps before becoming one of the intellectual leaders of the Prague Spring. His analysis of the deeper roots of the quasi-intellectual history of the Prague Spring is stimulating.

---

395 Günter Bishof, Stefan Karner and Peter Ruggenthaler, eds., *The Prague Spring and the Warsaw Pact Invasion of Czechoslovakia in 1968* (Lanham: Lexington Books, 2010).

396 See also Mark Kramer, "Die Sowjetunion, der Warschauer Pakt und blockinterne Krisen während der Breznev-Ära," in *Der Warschauer Pakt*, ed. Torsten Dietrich, Winfried Heinemann and Christian Ostermann (Berlin: Links, 2009), 273–336.

397 Konstantin Hermann, ed., *Sachsen und der Prager Frühling* (Beucha, Sax-Verlag, 2008), 67.

398 Martin Schulze Wessel, *Der Prager Frühling: Aufbruch in eine neue Welt* (Ditzingen: Reclam, 2018).

There were also some interesting contributions from Italian historians, chief among whom were Francesco Caccamo and Francesco Leoncini. Caccamo has published several works on the Prague Spring[399] but probably the most important is his recent *La Cecoslovacchia al tempo del socialismo reale* (2017).[400] Leoncini's long-term research interests lie in Central Europe.[401] He led a team which compiled a volume on Alexander Dubček and Jan Palach,[402] and more recently wrote a short biography of Dubček.[403] Also worthy of note are Enzo Bettiza's *La primavera di Praga. 1968: la rivoluzione dimenticata*,[404] and the volume edited by Santi Fedele and Pasquale Formaro published on the 40th anniversary of the invasion, which included chapters on some relatively neglected topics such as the impact of the events on Czechoslovak cinematography.[405] A research project at the University of Padua focused on the samizdat, but also necessarily touched on some aspects of the Prague Spring.[406]

The French historiography, traditionally more isolated, has dealt mainly with its own history of 1968 (civil unrest, demonstrations, major general strikes as well as the occupation of universities and factories across

---

399 For example, Francesco Caccamo, "Per la riforma del socialismo reale. Zdeněk Mlynář e il 'team' per lo sviluppo del Sistema politico," *Studi Storici* 57, no. 3 (2016): 669–708; Francesco Caccamo, Pavel Helan and Massimo Tria, eds., *Primavera di Praga, risveglio europeo* (Firenze: Firenze University Press, 2011).

400 Francesco Caccamo, *La Cecoslovacchia al tempo del socialismo reale: Regime, dissenso, esilio* (Roma: Società editrice Dante Alighieri, 2017).

401 Francesco Leoncini, *L'Europa centrale. Conflittualità e progetto. Passato e presente tra Praga, Budapest e Varsavia* (Venezia: Libreria Editrice Cafoscarina, 2003); see also, Francesco Leoncini, ed., *L'Europa del disincanto. Dal '68 praghese alla crisi del neoliberismo* (Soveria Mannelli: Rubbettino, 2011).

402 Francesco Leoncini, ed., *Alexander Dubcek e Jan Palach. Protagonisti della storia europea* (Soveria Mannelli: Rubbettino, 2008).

403 Francesco Leoncini, *Dubcek. Il socialismo della speranza. Immagini della Primavera cecoslovacca* (Roma: Gangemi, 2018).

404 Enzo Bettiza, *La primavera di Praga, 1968. La rivoluzione dimenticata* (Milano: Mondadori, 2008).

405 Santi Fedele and Pasquale Formaro, eds., *La Primavera di Praga: quarant'anni dopo* (Soveria Mannelli: Rubbettino, 2009).

406 Alessandro Catalano, "Il samizdat tradialogo e monologo: Le attività editoriali di Zdeněk Mlynář e la scelta degli interlocutori," *eSamizdat* (2010–2011): 261–280. A substantially expanded and reworked version of this article was also published in English. See Alessandro Catalano, "Zdeněk Mlynář and the search for socialist opposition from an active politician to a dissident to editorial work in exile," *Soudobé dějiny/Czech Journal of Contemporary History* III (2015): 90–156.

France in May). However, aside from the prominent historian of Central Europe mentioned several times already, Jackques Rupnik, other French academics addressed the Prague Spring and it would be a mistake to underplay, as we often do, the contribution of the French historiography to our understanding of the events. Apart from Rupnik, the journalist and political scientist François Fejtő devoted most of his career to a study of Eastern European regimes, including Czechoslovakia.[407]

More general works on Czechoslovak history have also appeared. Kevin McDermott shows how the historiography has moved from the ideological interpretations of the Cold War towards more serious analysis based on archive sources.[408] McDermott analyses the process of de-Stalinisation in Czechoslovakia, which slowly led to the Prague Spring and also addresses the Slovak question. He teamed up with Matthew Stibbe again in 2018 to edit a volume dedicated to responses to the Prague Spring in Eastern Europe.[409] The collection of thirteen essays explains why some regimes virulently opposed Dubček's reforms and encouraged the intervention while others stood apart.

Interest in the reforms of the Prague Spring, and in the invasion and its impact on Czechoslovakia, the Eastern bloc, the 'West' and Soviet foreign policy has certainly not faded away in recent years, especially during the 50th anniversary in 2018 when many new perspectives on old concepts were published. Drawing on interviews with around 100 Czechs and Slovaks, Thomas K. Murphy provided new perspectives on day-to-day life in Czechoslovakia, with chapters dedicated to the Prague Spring, the invasion, and the subsequent normalisation.[410] Fresh takes on the subject are still appearing, such as that of Melanie Brand, who examines the impact of cognitive bias on the analytical output of the US intelligence agency during the Prague Spring.[411]

---

407 François Fejtö and Jacques Rupnik, eds., *Le Printemps tchéchoslovaque 1968* (Paris: Editions Complexes, 1999).
408 Kevin McDermott, *Communist Czechoslovakia, 1945–89: A Political and Social History* (London: Palgrave, 2015).
409 Kevin McDermott and Matthew Stibbe, eds., *Eastern Europe in 1968. Responses to the Prague Spring and Warsaw Pact Invasion* (London: Palgrave, 2018).
410 Thomas Murphy, *Czechoslovakia Behind the Curtain: Life, Work and Culture in the Communist Era* (Jefferson: McFarland & Co., 2018).
411 Melanie Brand, "Mind games: Cognitive bias, US intelligence and the 1968 Soviet invasion of Czechoslovakia," *Intelligence and National Security* (2019), 1–15.

The Prague Spring and its aftermath is one of the most thoroughly researched events in the whole of Czechoslovak history. While the level of research is very high, some questions remain unanswered. There is an ongoing discussion about the reasons for the intervention and about the nature of the Prague Spring and whether we should speak of 'reforms' or a 'revolution'.[412] With the obvious exceptions of Skilling, Williams, Rupnik and others, Western historians often fail to exploit the full potential of the Czech and Slovak historiography and its interpretations and confine themselves to a very limited number of Czech and Slovak works and sources. This is especially true of Slovak research, which is almost unknown in the West. For example, while the economic reforms of the Czechoslovak economists have been described and analysed exhaustingly, the Western historiography has almost completely ignored economic development in Slovakia. There are reasons for this failure of the West to connect with 'Czechoslovak' research. The main problem with the Czech and especially the Slovak historiography and research is a lack of 'internationalisation'. Very few works are published in world languages such as English, German, French or Russian, and academics from both the Czech Republic and Slovakia tend to pass over the latest methodological approaches and interpretations of the Western historiography and fail to place their research within the international context. The Prague Spring is a very popular topic in the Czech and Slovak historiography. Quantitatively it is extensively treated—there are hundreds of works. But only minimal emphasis is placed on conceptual questions, and Czech and Slovak historians often lack the methodological apparatus for deeper and more precise analysis.

Another problem of the historiography of the Czechoslovak crisis of 1968 is the secrecy surrounding Soviet policymaking and the role of Eastern European leaders such as Ulbricht and Kádár. The problem is often identified as the 'hermetic seal' on Soviet records and the lack of access to Russian archives. While this is generally true, some archives are in fact accessible. For example, transcripts of meetings of the Politburo of the CPSU pertaining to the 1968 crisis are available at the Cold War Studies archive at Harvard University; many of the files from the Ukrainian archives are

---

412 These are well summed up in Lyons, *Mass and Elite Attitudes*, 258–264, and particulary in the table on 262—although only Czech and English literature is consulted.

also accessible.[413] The diaries of Petro Shelest, the First Secretary of the Ukrainian Communist Party, are available in the Russian State Archives. Shelest was a key figure during the Czechoslovak crisis and with some notable exceptions (such as Mark Kramer) few authors have used his diaries and other materials. Some important new insights into the decision-making process in Moscow were brought to light by R. G. Pikhoia,[414] who worked with the documents of the Central Committee of the Communist Party of the Soviet Union. Until more Russian archives are opened up, however, we cannot know the precise answers to many questions. One thing that is not in doubt is that new scholarly discussions and further research on the Prague Spring will appear in the future.[415]

---

[413] Mark Kramer, "Ukraine and the Soviet-Czechoslovak crisis of 1968 (Part 2): New evidence from the Ukrainian archives," *Cold War International History Project Bulletin*, no. 14/15 (2003): 273–368. For an analysis of the Ukrainian historiography dealing with the Prague Spring, see Ruslan Postolovskyj and Andrij Slesarenko, "'Празька весна' 1968 року в Чехословаччині в українській історіографії," Міжнародні зв'язки України: наукові пошуки і знахідки 27 (2018), 106–119.

[414] R. G. Pikhoia, "Czechoslovakia 1968: A view from Moscow according to Central Committee documents," *Russian Studies in History* 44, no. 3 (2014): 35–80.

[415] This essay is slightly updated and revised version of my article previously published in Slovak as: Jakub Drábik, "Pražská jar a invázia vojsk Varšavskej zmluvy do Československa v roku 1968 očami "západnej" historiografie," *Historický časopis* 68, no. 4 (2020): 693–721.

11
Conclusion

The Prague spring and the August 1968 occupation of Czechoslovakia by the Warsaw pact armies never ceases to inspire the historical research, nor the public debate. According to the most recent polls, from March 2018, the August 1968 occupation is perceived negatively by 61% of Slovaks and 76% of Czechs. Only 9 % of Slovaks and 5 % of Czechs consider the invasion a positive thing.[416] These results make the 1968 occupation the worst event in history according to Slovaks, ahead of Vladmír Mečiar's era of 1994 to 1998 (59% perceived this negatively), the February 1948 communist coup d'état (46%) and the wartime Slovak regime (46%).[417] Similarly, the 1968 occupation is perceived by Czechs to be the worst event in history, ahead of the period of the Protectorate Bohemia and Moravia (74%), the signing of the Munich agreement (69%) and the February 1948 Communist coup d'état (67%).[418]

However, ss Jacques Rupnik concluded in his study, the significance of the Prague Spring cannot be measured only by its defeat. Its contribution should be understood in the interplay between its Czecho-Slovak and European dimensions. The August '68 invasion might not have provoked a major international crisis, but it certainly was an important part of the year that shook Europe. The Soviet occupation of Czechoslovakia ended the illusion that Communism could be reformed, that the ideals of democratic pluralism are compatible with Marxism and that Stalinism had been nothing more than just a wrong turn. Dubček's reforms were in fact not the beginning, but the end. Frome then on, radicals and reformers not just in Czechoslovakia, but in other Soviet satellites stopped looking to the

---

416 Zora Bútorová—Grigorij Mesežnikov. Osudové osmičky vo vedomí slovenskej spolčonosti. Bratislava: Inštitút pre verejné otázky, 2018, p. 61. Accesible online: http://www.ivo.sk/buxus/docs//publikacie/subory/Osudove_osmicky.pdf
417 Zor Bútorová, a—Grigorij Mesežnikov. Osudové osmičky vo vedomí slovenskej spolčonosti. Bratislava: Inštitút pre verejné otázky, 2018, p. 61. Accesible online, p. 54
418 Centrum pro výzkum veřejného mínění, Občané o osobnostech, obdobích a událostech česko-slovenské historie od vzniku ČSR po súčasnost—březen 2018. Accesible online: https://cvvm.soc.cas.cz/media/com_form2content/documents/c2/a4607/f9/pd180509.pdf

Party as a vehicle for their aspirations. As the articles in this book suggest, the same was clear also in other Eastern block countries.

In Hungary, the party leadership concluded what they already knew after the 1956 revolution: adjusting to the aims of an empire does not allow the subordinate countries to enact autonomous policy. While János Kádár initially supported Alexander Dubček, this support soon faded and the MSZMP approved the participation of the Hungarian army to participate in the military intervention. In Poland, Władysław Gomułka, for reasons evident to him, supported the aggression to Czechoslovakia with vigour. He not only had a critical attitude towards Dubček, but also to his successor, accusing him of too slow progress of the normalization policy that came after invasion. As Mirosław Szumiło concluded in his chapter, we cannot precisely determine the distribution of individual attitudes towards the invasion in Polish society, but the condemnation of the aggression and outrage towards it clearly dominated the public discourse in the first days after invasion. This, however, soon changed too, as a result of propaganda, and the circle of people accepting the intervention gradually grew.

A similar situation occurred in other Easter Block countries. One of the key consequences of what has happened in Czechoslovakia was the gradual and almost invisible but irreversible process of erosion of the tacit consensus reached at that time about the legitimacy of the regime in Bulgaria itself. Slow breakdown between the intelligentsia and the party bureaucracy started as well. As Bulgarian dissident writer Georgi Markov, quoted by Mihail Gruev in his chapter concluded, "for all those who had taken the Aurora's gunshot as the birth moment of ideals, hopes, illusions, dreams of some vaguely beautiful, new human life, for those who fanatically preserved this feeling throughout so many painful years, the date of August 21 was the end." From now on, Communism in Eastern Europe as a whole was sustained only by foreign loans and the Soviet military.

One of the most interesting reactions to the invasion occurred in Yugoslavia, as analysed by Ljubodrag Dimić. Yugoslav party and state leadership paid close attention to the events in Czechoslovakia long before the invasion. Yugoslavs were not only concerned about the internal developments in Czechoslovakia, they were convinced that the way Moscow and other Eastern European capitals would react to the events in the CSSR could challenge and even endanger some of the basic principles of Yugoslavia's foreign policy, specifically the non-interference in other countries' internal affairs above others. After his visit to Moscow in April 1968, it became clear to Tito, that some of Brezhnev's remarks on the situation in Czechoslovakia could be understood as an implicit critique of Yugoslavia's foreign political line. The Soviet leader assumed that the situation in Czechoslovakia could trigger a "chain reaction" in other socialist countries, including Yugoslavia. What he demanded from Tito was a "closer alliance" between the two countries, which in this case meant a common stance towards Czechoslovakia and Soviets attempted to make Yugoslavia at least indirectly involved in the forthcoming intervention.

Tito and other leading Yugoslav communists, however, rejected the claims that the military intervention was caused by the need to defend the western borders of Czechoslovakia. The reasons behind the 'occupation' of Czechoslovakia were in their opinion both political and ideological in nature. Tito was convinced that the Eastern Bloc countries considered Yugoslavia to be the main inspirator, initiator and protagonist of what was going on in Prague, and that therefore the main target of the attack was Yugoslavia itself. He further stated that the intervention was a warning to other Socialist countries as well

Tito's protest against the military intervention in Czechoslovakia was at the same time a call to defend Yugoslavia. By declaratively protecting the general principles of international relations and reaffirming the interests of world socialism, Tito was in the first place trying to defend the internal and foreign political position of his own country. He considered the intervention in Czechoslovakia to be a threat to 'the very independence of our country', and therefore appealed to his compatriots to 'remain calm', 'to prevent panic and unrest', but to make clear to all potential aggressors that the Yugoslavs would defend their own country until the end. Military readiness was raised to the highest level, party propaganda successfully harnessed the patriotic feelings amongst the Yugoslav communists to bolster its ranks. Although in late 1968 internal Yugoslav reports concluded that the threat from the USSR was "real", during the spring of 1969 the assessments began to change.

Alexander Stykalin, on the other hand, explained in his part the views of the Soviet leadership. As for Brezhnev, caution and indecisiveness were fully manifested in all his activities before intervention, but he, along with the whole leadership of the USSR without exception agreed that it was necessary to put an end to the reform processes in Czechoslovakia, since such reforms were bound to lead to a weakening of the monopoly power of the Communist elite. The disagreements were only about assessing the methods of action.

The unexpected development in Czechoslovakia, despite the condemnation of the invasion, did not endanger the American policy of 'building the bridges' with Central Europe and replacing the Cold War confrontation by cooperation and mutual safety of the superpowers, as explained by Slavomir Michalek in his chapter. The invasion was concluded without any direct intervention from the USA. President Richard Nixon's administration, that took the office in January 1969, followed the steps of Lyndon Johnson and refused to do anything that would be an intervention in the internal affairs of the Soviet camp.

As the chapters in this volume have shown, the situation, reasons for the participation in the aggression, and events leading up to the decision to participate or abstain from it, were very different and very complex in every country. 50 years after the events of August 1968 and despite the vastness of existing literature on the subject, many questions remain unanswered and further research, especially with the emphasis on the conceptual questions, transnational histories and interpretation, is needed. Similarly, we need to move from isolated historical narratives of national historiographies towards more cross-border cooperation between scholars dealing with such complex questions. This book represents a small step along that path.

Selected Sources

Archives

Archiwum Instytutu Pamięci Narodowej (Archive of the Institute of National Remembrance, AIPN)

Archiv Ministerstva zahraničních věcí České republiky (The Archives of the Ministry of Foreign Affairs of the Czech Republic, AMZV ČR)

Archiwum Akt Nowych w Warszawie (The Central Archives of Modern Records in Warsaw, AAN)

Magyar Nemzeti Levéltár (National Archives of Hungary, MNL)

Muzej istorije Jugoslavije (The Museum of Yugoslav History, MIJ)

National Archives and Records (NAR), National Czech and Slovak Museum and Library (NCSML)

Národní archiv ČR (National Archives of the Czech Republic, NAČR)

Tsentralen dŭrzhaven arkhiv (Bulgarian Central State Archive, CSA)

Literature

BAKALOV, Ivan. *Furst-Person Putsch Makers. The Plots Against Todor Zhivkov*. Sofia: Millenium, 2008.

BETTIZA, Enzo. *La primavera di Praga, 1968. La rivoluzione dimenticata*. Milano: Mondadori, 2008.

BISHOF, Günter—KARNER, Stefan Karner—RUGGENTHALER, Peter (eds.), *The Prague Spring and the Warsaw Pact Invasion of Czechoslovakia in 1968*. Lanham: Lexington Books, 2010.

BLAŽEK, Petr—KAMIŃSKI, Łukasz—VÉVODA, Rudolf (eds.): Polsko a Československo w roce 1968. Sborník příspěvků z mezinárodní vědecké konference. Praha: Dokořán, 2006.

BOHLEN, Charles E. *Witness to History 1929–1969*. New York: W.W. Norton and Company Inc., 1973.

BRACKE, Maud. *Which Socialism? Whose Détente? West European Communism and the Czechoslovak Crisis of 1968*. Budapest: Central European Press, 2007.

BRUS, Włodzimierz—KENDE, Pierre—MLYNÁŘ, Zdeněk (eds.), *"Normalisierungsprozesse" im sowjetisierten Mitteleuropa: Ungarn, Tschechoslowakei, Polen*. Köln: Index, 1982.

Selected Sources

BROWN, Archie—GRAY, Jack (ed.). *Political Culture in Communist States.* London: Macmillan, 1977.

CACCAMO, Francesco. *La Cecoslovacchia al tempo del socialismo reale: Regime, dissenso, esilio.* Roma: Società editrice Dante Alighieri, 2017.

CACCAMO, Francesco. "Per la riforma del socialismo reale. Zdeněk Mlynář e il 'team' per lo sviluppo del Sistema politico," *Studi Storici* 57, no. 3 (2016): 669–708.

DAWISHA, Karen. *The Kremlin and the Prague Spring.* Los Angeles: University of California Press, 1984.

DAWISHA, Karen—HANSON, Philip (eds.). *Soviet-East European Dilemmas: Coercion, Competition, and Consent.* New York: Holmes & Meier, 1981.

DIMIĆ, Ljubodrag. Yugoslavia and Security in Europe during the 1960s. Views, Attitudes, Initiatives. In *Токови историје*, 2016/3, 9–42.

DOKTOROV, Mihail. In a Fight with the Octopus. The "Second Center" in the Sruggle against Zhivkovists 1965–1968. Sofia, Kota, 1993.

DUBČEK, Alexander: *Naděje umírá poslední. Vlastní životopis Alexandra Dubčeka.* Praha: Svoboda-Libertas, 1993.

EIDLIN, Fred. *The Logic of "Normalisation": The Soviet Intervention in Czechoslovakia of 21 August 1968 and the Czechoslovak Response.* Boulder: East European Monographs, 1980.

EISLER, Jerzy: *Polski rok 1968.* Warszawa: Instytut Pamięci Narodowej, 2006.

EISLER, Jerzy et al.: Aparat bezpieczeństwa, propaganda a Praska Wiosna. Zbiór materiałów z konferencji międzynarodowej Praga, 7–9 września 2008 r. Praga: Ústav pro Studium Totalitních Režimů, 2009.

FURET, François. *L'Enigme de la désagrégation communiste.* Paris: Fondation Saint Simon, 1990.

GARLICKI, Andrzej—PACZKOWSKI, Andrzej (eds.): *Zaciskanie pętli. Tajne dokumenty dotyczące Czechosłowacji 1968.* Warszawa: Wydawnictwo Sejmowe, 1995.

GITELMAN, Zvi. "The politics of socialist restoration in Hungary and Czechoslovakia," *Comparative Politics* 13, no. 2 (1981): 187–210.

GOLAN, Galia. "Antonin Novotny: The sources and nature of his power," *Canadian Slavonic Papers* 14, no. 3 (1972): 421–441.

GOLAN, Galia. *Reform Rule in Czechoslovakia: The Dubček Era, 1968–1969.* Cambridge: Cambridge University Press, 1973.

GÜNTER, Bischof—KARNER, Stefan—RUGGENTHALER, Peter (eds). *The Prague Spring and the Warsaw Pact invasion of Czechoslovakia in 1968.* Lanham: Lexington Books, 2010.

HABERMAS, Jürgen. *Die nachholende Revolution: Kleine Plotisiche Schriften VII.* Frankfurt: Suhrkamp Verlag, 1990.

HUGHES, Geraint. "British policy towards Eastern Europe and the impact of the 'Prague Spring', 1964-68," *Cold War History* 4, no. 2 (2004): 115-139.

KAPLAN, Karel. *Political Persecution in Czechoslovakia, 1948-1972.* Köln: Index, 1983.

KAPLAN, Karel. *Winter into Spring: The Czechoslovak Press and the Reform Movement 1963-1968.* New York: Columbia University Press, 1977.

KARABEL, Jerome. "The revolt of intellectuals: The origins of the Prague Spring and the politics of reform communism," *Research in Social Movements* 18, no. 1 (1995): 93-143.

KARNER, Stefan et al., *Prager Frühling. Das internationale Krisenjahr 1968.* Köln: Böhlau, 2008.

KOWALSKI, Lech: *Kryptonim "Dunaj". Udział wojsk polskich w interwencji zbrojnej w Czechosłowacji w 1968 roku.* Warszawa: Książka i Wiedza 1992.

KRAMER, Mark. "New sources on the 1968 Soviet invasion of Czechoslovakia," *Cold War International History Project Bulletin*, no. 2 (1992): 1-19.

KRAMER, Mark. "The Prague Spring and the Soviet invasion of Czechoslovakia: New interpretations," *Cold War International History Project Bulletin*, no. 3 (1993): 1-13.

KREJČÍ, Jaroslav. *Social Change and Stratification in Post-War Czechoslovakia.* London: Macmillan, 1972.

KUSIN, Vladimir. *From Dubček to Charter 77. A Study of "Normalization" in Czechoslovakia 1968-1978.* New York: St. Martin's Press, 1978.

KUSIN, Vladimír. *The Intellectual Origins of the Prague Spring: The Development of Reformist Ideas in Czechoslovakia 1956-1967.* New York: Cambridge University Press, 1971.

LEONCINI, Francesco. *Dubcek. Il socialismo della speranza. Immagini della Primavera cecoslovacca.* Roma: Gangemi, 2018.

LITTLE, Robert (ed.). *The Czech Black Book: An Eyewitness, Documented Account of the Invasion of Czechoslovakia.* New York: Frederick A. Praeger, 1969; London: Pall Mall, 1969.

MACHÁČEK, Michal. *Gustáv Husák.* Praha: Vyšehrad, 2017.

MAJOROV, Alexandr. *Vtorženie Čechoslovakia.* Moskva: Izdateľstvo "Prava čeloveka", 1998.

MARKOV, Georgi. *New in Abstentia Reports for Bulgaria.* Sofia, Bulgarski pisatel, 1991.

Selected Sources

MCDERMOTT, Kevin. *Communist Czechoslovakia, 1945–89: A Political and Social History*. London: Palgrave, 2015.

MCDERMOTT, Kevin—STIBBE, Matthew (eds.) *Revolution and Resistance in Eastern Europe: Challenges to Communist Rule*. Oxford: Berg, 2006.

MILLER, James E. (ed.). Foreign Relations of the United States (further FRUS) 1964–1968, Volume XVII, Eastern Europe. Washington: United States Government Printing Office, 1996.

MLYNÁŘ, Zdeněk. *Night Frost in Prague: The End of Humane Socialism*. London: C. Hurst, 1980.

NAVRÁTIL, Jaromír et al., *The Prague Spring 1968: A National Security Archive Documents Reader*. Budapest: Central European University Press, 1998.

Operace "Dunaj": *vojáci a Pražské jaro 1968: studie a dokumenty*. Praha: ÚSD AV ČR, 1994.

PAJÓREK, Leszek: *Polska a "Praska Wiosna". Udział Wojska Polskiego w interwencji zbrojnej w Czechosłowacji w 1968 roku*. Warsawa: Wojskowy Instytut Historyczny, 1998.

PAUL, David. *The Cultural Limits of Revolutionary Politics: Change and Continuity in Socialist Czechoslovakia*. Boulder: East European Monogaphs, 1979.

PELIKÁN, Jiří. *Ici Prague—l'opposition interieure*. Paris: Seuil, 1973.

PETRANOVIĆ, Branko. *The Yugoslav Experience of Serbian National Integration*, New York: Boulder 2002.

PITHART, Peter. *1968—A Memoir of the Prague Spring*. Budapest: Central European University Press, 1998.

"Pražskaja vesna" i meždunarodnyj krizis 1968 goda. Moskva: Institut všeobščej istorii RAN, Demokratia, 2010.

POVOLNÝ, Daniel. *Operace Dunaj. Krvavá odpoveď Varšavské smlouvy na pražské jaro 1968*. Praha: Akademia, 2018.

Public Papers of the Presidents of United States, Lyndon B. Johnson. Public Messages, Speeches and Statements of the President, 1963–1969. Washington DC: United States Government Printing Office, 1970.

RAKOWSKI, Mieczysław: Dzienniki polityczne 1967–1968. Warszawa: Iskry, 1999.

ROKICKI, Konrad—STĘPIEŃ, Sławomir (eds.): *Oblicza Marca 1968*. Warszawa: Instytut Pamięci Narodowej 2004.

RUCHNIEWICZ, Krzysztof—SZAYNOK, Bożena—TYSZKIEWICZ, Jakub (eds.): *Między Październikiem a Grudniem. Polityka zagraniczna doby Gomułki*. Toruń: Wydawnictwo Adam Marszałek, 2005.

Selected Sources

RUPNIK, Jacques—FEJTÖ, François (eds.) *Le Printemps tchéchoslovaque 1968.* Paris: Editions Complexes, 1999.

SKILLING, Gordon. *Czechoslovakia's Interrupted Revolution.* Princeton: Princeton University Press, 1976.

SKILLING, Gordon. "Journey to Czechoslovakia: Spring 1968," *Kosmas: Czechoslovak and Central European Journal* 11, no. 1 (Summer 1992): 27–42.

SKILLING, Gordon. "Reform aborted: Czechoslovakia in retrospect," *International Journal* 28, no. 3 (1973), p. 431–445.

STOLARIK, Mark. *The Prague Spring and the Warsaw Pact Invasion of Czechoslovakia, 1968. Forty Years Later.* Mundelein: Bolchazy-Carducci, 2010.

SVITÁK, Ivan. *The Czechoslovak Experiment: 1968–1969* (New York: Columbia University Press, 1971).

ŠIMEČKA, Milan. *The Restoration of Order: The Normalization of Czechoslovakia, 1969–1976.* London: Verso, 1984.

TIGRID, Pavel. *La chute irresistible d'Alexander Dubček* (Paris: Calmann-Levy, 1969).

TIGRID, Pavel. *Le printempts de Prague* (Paris: Editions du Seuil, 1968).

VALENTA, Jiří. "Revolutionary change, Soviet intervention, and 'Normalization' in East-Central Europe," *Comparative Politics* 16, no. 2 (1984): 127–151.

VALENTA, Jiří. *Soviet Intervention in Czechoslovakia, 1968. Anatomy of a Decision* (Baltimore: The Johns Hopkins University Press, 1979).

VONDROVÁ, Jitka, NAVRÁTIL, Jaromír. *Mezinárodní souvislosti československé krize 1967–1970. Červenec-srpen 1968.* Brno: Doplněk, 1996.

WESSEL, Martin Schulze. *Der Prager Frühling: Aufbruch in eine neue Welt.* Ditzingen: Reclam, 2018.

WILLIAMS, Kieran. *The Prague Spring and its Aftermath. Czechoslovak Politics, 1968–1970.* Cambridge: Cambridge University Press, 1997.

WINDSOR, Philip—ROBERTS, Adam. *Czechoslovakia, 1968: Reform, Repression, Resistance.* New York: Columbia University Press, 1969.